Challenging the Scho Agenda in Early Childhood Education

MW00963091

Challenging the normative paradigm that school readiness is a positive and necessary objective for all young children, this book asserts that the concept is a deficit-based practice that fosters the continuation of discriminatory classifications. Tager draws on findings of a qualitative study to reveal how the neoliberal agenda of school reform based on high-stakes testing sorts and labels children as non-ready, affecting their overall schooling careers. Tager reflects critically on the relationship between race and school readiness, showing how the resulting exclusionary measures perpetuate the marginalization of low-income Black children from an early age. Disrupting expected notions of readiness is imperative to ending practices of structural classism and racism in early childhood education.

Miriam B. Tager is Assistant Professor of Early Childhood Education at Westfield State University, USA.

Routledge Research in Early Childhood Education

This series provides a platform for researchers to present their latest research and discuss key issues in Early Childhood Education.

Books in the series include:

Children as Citizens
Engaging with the child's voice in educational settings
Pauline Harris and Harry Manatakis

Early Years Second Language Education
International perspectives on theory and practice
Edited by Sandie Mourão and Mónica Lourenço

iPads in the Early Years
Developing literacy and creativity
Michael Dezuanni, Karen Dooley, Sandra Gattenhof and Linda Knight

Teaching for Active Citizenship
Research insights from the fields of teaching moral values and personal epistemology in early years classrooms
Joanne Lunn Brownlee, Susan Walker, Eva Johansson and Laura Scholes

Early Childhood Education Management
Insights from practice
Mary Moloney and Jan Pettersen

Early Childhood Education for Muslim Children
Rationales and practices in South Africa
Hasina Banu Ebrahim

An Interdisciplinary Approach to Early Childhood Education and Care
Perspectives from Australia
Susanne Garvis and Matthew Manning

Challenging the School Readiness Agenda in Early Childhood Education
Miriam B. Tager

Challenging the School Readiness Agenda in Early Childhood Education

Miriam B. Tager

Routledge
Taylor & Francis Group

LONDON AND NEW YORK

First published 2017 by Routledge

2 Park Square, Milton Park, Abingdon, Oxfordshire OX14 4RN
52 Vanderbilt Avenue, New York, NY 10017

Routledge is an imprint of the Taylor & Francis Group, an informa business

First issued in paperback 2018

Library of Congress Cataloguing-in-Publication Data
A catalog record for this book has been requested

ISBN: 978-1-138-67239-0 (hbk)
ISBN: 978-0-367-19582-3 (pbk)

Typeset in Sabon
by Apex CoVantage, LLC

To: Lina, Derek, Billy, Michael and Jay (not their real names) and all young low-income Black children who are daily identified as non-school ready and have this stigma follow them around for their entire school lives.

Contents

Preface

There is a long-standing notion within the early childhood research community that *school readiness* is a positive and necessary objective for all young children (preschool–first grade) to attain. If children are ready for school, maintains this research, then they fare better in school and lead more productive economic lives. School readiness is defined as children being able to adapt to school culture successfully and therefore ready to learn. My research challenges this normative paradigm by asserting that in actuality, the concept of *school readiness* and all that it encompasses is a deficit-based practice that fosters discriminatory practices toward low-income Black children. Teachers, now more than ever, due to higher demands/expectations, are being forced to push *school readiness* practices inside the classroom, and this is detrimental to their pedagogical practices. This fosters an expectation of inappropriate practices, pushing down the curriculum and expanding the gap between White middle class children and low-income Black children.

The classification of *school readiness* in children also reinforces a system of syphoning off children perceived as non-school ready (into special education) and labeling them as 'at-risk' and below average learners. There are perceived differences in the values, knowledge systems and socio-cultural beliefs between the philosophies employed by White middle class educators (the normative discourse of schools) and those upheld by differing Black populations. This leads to the further marginalization of these cultures, as White teachers refer large numbers of these children labeled non-school ready to special education, usually up to 30 to 50% of their classrooms (Harry & Klingner, 2006).

This book focuses on the lives of classified non-school ready children, who are low-income and Black (four out of five are boys) and are not able to master the tasks/assessments assigned by the increased standards of the Core Curriculum. They are directly affected by this push for *school readiness*, as they are quickly classified as deficient learners who are not able to 'do school' properly. This, in turn, leads to exclusionary measures, as they are sorted and labeled as non-ready. All five children in my study have since left regular education classrooms after kindergarten or first grade, thus affecting their overall schooling career. Three are presently in inclusion classrooms, one is in an ELL classroom and the other is in a special education classroom.

Therefore, this label of being non-school ready has largely impacted their futures as students in the American school system.

Through the eyes of these non-school ready children, I will clearly show how this quick classification process works within the kindergarten and first grade classroom. The pressure to sort children within the first weeks of school is so great that teachers unknowingly are perpetuating this exclusionary process without noticing that these children are usually low-income Black children. Furthermore, they are not differentiating between Black populations, and therefore are perpetuating a color-blind discourse. This reveals one of the key problems of the American school system, including early childhood programs, which is the continuing practice of structural racism. This book controversially challenges the American neoliberal agenda of school reform based on standardized testing, and combats these ongoing deficit practices in the early childhood classroom.

There are very few books within this field that give a true inside view of the specific practices involved in the classification of *school readiness* in a young child. This book shows how young Black children are given very little time to adjust to the culture of the school. They are categorized as working too slowly, as being a behavior problem, uncooperative, non-verbal and other specific non-school ready factors, which directly relates to their future schooling career. Therefore, these practices perpetuate the ongoing theory of Black children as being 'culturally deprived' and 'disadvantaged' in some way. It is imperative that early childhood educators critically reflect on this normative practice and challenge its very existence so that we can effectively address these exclusionary measures in our classrooms and schools.

It is important to note that all the names of the children and teacher participants have been changed. The school, the district and the geographical location have also not been identified, except to say that this location is a part of the larger tri-state area of New York City. All identifying markers and descriptions of the participants and the area have been eradicated so that the participants maintain their privacy. This is just one public school district in the North East and is not meant to be indicative of the entire American school system, although there may be some consistent themes in other schools surrounding this issue.

It also should be mentioned that I am aware that I, even as a critical educator, hold certain values/perceptions related to being a White person. Even as I reflect on this, I realize that I can't be, as an insider to this study, completely objective or neutral on this topic. I, therefore, must consistently remind myself and the reader that I am a White person, and even with awareness of this, I am still holding onto my White privilege. I acknowledge this White privilege and all that it entails in the world, and it propels me to look more closely at spaces that reproduce racist structures.

This book is written primarily for undergraduate/graduate students in the field of early childhood education and can be utilized in conjunction with other critical texts that challenge dominant ideologies in the field. It will be helpful for early childhood researchers and fellow academic scholars both nationally and internationally.

The following is a brief overview of what to expect in this book:

Chapter One, **Introducing the Non-School Ready Child**, introduces the five children in this study along with the research methodology and practices that reveal this deficit practice/identification.

Chapter Two, **The Historical Context of the Non-School Ready Child**, delves into the deficit history of early childhood education programs and the theory of culturally deprivation. It also provides a direct connection to the neoliberal movement in education and how the standards/testing movement relates to this deficit classification.

Chapter Three, **The Ecology of School Readiness**, reveals the identification process of being labeled non-school ready. Teachers have specific expectations, including the ability of the child to follow school culture, utilize appropriate socio-emotional responses and work efficiently.

Chapter Four, **Higher Demands: Putting Pressure on the Identified Non-School Ready Child**, expands on the last chapter by specifically revealing how higher demands (from Common Core objectives/practices) negatively impact the pedagogical practices of developmentally appropriate work with young children.

Chapter Five, **Blaming the Parents**, challenges the notion of parents being to blame for a child being classified as non-school ready. These children's parents are working three and four jobs trying to make a living wage and cannot always conform to specific school involvement times. The differing cultural expectations of school also play a role in the blaming.

Chapter Six, **Young Black Lives Matter**, powerfully exposes how race plays a role in the classification of school readiness. These non-ready children are all Black and hail from a variety of cultures (Haitian, African American, African, etc.). Their teachers (all White and middle class) are uncomfortable discussing race and pedagogical practices related to race and are unable to distinguish between various cultural backgrounds within their Black populations. Race and meritocracy and issues of race combined with socio-economic class are covered as well.

Chapter Seven, **Inequities and Inequalities in Early Childhood Programs**, reveals the overall racist and classist structure that surrounds this issue. Inequities within the district prevail as well as obvious inequalities, including: differences in substitute teachers, technology systems, libraries, fundraising and etc.

Chapter Eight, **A Call for Action**, calls for a challenge to the normative practices of *school readiness*. It reveals what happened to these non-ready children and how we, as early childhood teachers, can learn from these ongoing deficit practices. Included is a sample letter to the local school district specifying exactly how to combat the deficient nature of *school readiness* identification.

It is an honor to contribute to the research in this area, and I can only hope that this controversial book makes an impact on the dominant philosophy of *school readiness* and changes how educators view the topic.

Acknowledgements

Robin, thank you for letting me spend time in the library even when you needed a break from the girls. You are nurturing, supportive, creative and a wonderful life partner. I know it was especially hard after the long hours in writing my dissertation to have me write another book so soon. You totally get me, and that is only one of the reasons why I adore you.

Ella and Lily are the stars in my eyes and give me hope for this world. Ella, you are one of the most interesting people I have ever met, and you continually surprise me with your insight and knowledge of this world. Lily, I know I am supposed to be an expert at your age group (preschool), but you challenge my thoughts about preschoolers daily, and I appreciate it. I also thank you both for coming to visit my classes each semester to be real world examples of wonderfully creative students with individual educational plans.

Thank you to my dissertation committee at the CUNY Graduate Center, but especially to my advisor, Dr. Wendy Luttrell, for all the wonderful support and feedback.

I want to acknowledge my wonderful working environment. To all my colleagues at Westfield State University, thank you for your encouragement and support, including: Ramon, Drew, Juanita, Errold, Wilma, Nitza, Laura, Megan, B. J., Sandy, David, Jim, Kathy I., Robin, Stephanie, Trudy and Kathy T. A special thanks goes to my mentor, and Early Childhood comrade, Dr. Terri Griffin.

Thank you Karen Adler, my editor at Routledge, for answering all my questions with a warm heart and open mind. You have been a joy to work with and you made it so easy to complete this project.

My friends are what continually keep me going, so thank you for all the phone calls, texts and in person support. A big shout out to Juanita P., Mark W., Maria P., Rondi S. and Ramon V.

I also need to recognize the love and support of my family, including my parents, who are retired academics, Jack and Florence. Thank you to my siblings, David, Dan, Liz and to my nieces, Olive, Ana, Laila and nephew Alex.

Thank you Smith Library for being my home away from home and for being such a quiet place to write and think. You will forever be my 'sweet escape.'

Finally, I need to thank every pre-k, k and first-grade teacher teaching in the American urban public schools. You give me the motivation and strength to persevere and commit to actively fighting for much needed policy changes in Early Childhood Education.

1   Introducing the Non-School Ready Child

"Lina, are you with me?" Ms. Franklin calls from the front of the rug.

Lina is sitting by the bookshelf, off to the left side of the teacher. Her brown chemically straightened hair is sticking out on both sides of her head and the rest is pulled back with a black hair tie. She is wearing a sweater dress with colorful zigzags. Her first grade teacher, Ms. Franklin, is sitting on a blue cushioned rocking chair around five feet away, next to a free standing wooden easel with chart paper on it.

Lina is moving around, twisting her head and looking everywhere. She looks down at the rug. She does not look at Ms. Franklin. Ms. Franklin has a globe in her lap and is describing it to the class.

"Many years ago the Inuit nation crossed over into Alaska . . ."

"From the North," calls out a boy.

Ms. Franklin holds up the Do Not Interrupt sign. "Remember not to call out," she says. Other children raise their hands. Lina does not. Ms. Franklin calls on another boy with reddish hair, who talks about the Inuits moving to Alaska to set up their homes. After a few minutes Ms. Franklin turns to Lina and again says,

"Lina are you with me?"

Lina looks up but still does not look at the teacher. She rocks sideways on her butt. She looks at the chart paper as Ms. Franklin starts to write with a marker. Lina is not raising her hand. She is not smiling. She looks around the room as others respond to Ms. Franklin. Ms. Franklin fills out the chart with their responses. Lina flattens her hair with her hand. Pieces of her hair stick right back up. She yawns as she moves her head up to look at the ceiling. She pulls at her hair. She takes out the hair tie from the back and pulls her hair tight, trying to smooth out the sides. She puts the hair tie on again.

"Lina what did they used to do when they cut holes in the ice?" Ms. Franklin says suddenly, staring right at her. Everyone turns to look at her. There is a pause.

"Fish," she says, her hands are still in her hair, smoothing out the sides. She takes out the tie again and shakes her hair out. She puts a clip in the front and puts the hair tie on her wrist. She holds her nose with her two index fingers and then strokes her hair again. Now Ms. Franklin is asking

about the environment. Her right arm goes up, stretching it back to her neck. Ms. Franklin notices and thinks she is raising her hand.

"Lina . . . (pause) do you know what I mean?"

"No," Lina says as she shakes her head. Lina plays with the tie on her wrist.

"Hold on," Ms. Franklin says to the class as they talk and move around, "I know I am keeping you at the rug too long . . . you will go back in a minute."

"Lina who does it harm? If ice is melting . . ."

"The one with the big . . ." Lina starts.

"Big what?" asks Ms. Franklin.

"Polar bears," says Lina.

"Why?" The teacher looks around for another person to answer.

"I am going to see if you are listening about now and then," says Ms. Franklin. She is looking at Lina. She then opens a book and shows a picture of an oil field.

"What is the problem that affects the Inuit culture?" she asks.

A boy calls out.

"Why are you raising your hand if you are calling out at the same time?" Lina is leaning against the bookshelf now.

"Drilling for oil. What do you think it does to the land and to animals?"

Ms. Franklin leans in over a girl with long brown hair. "Sit nicely. . . . What do you think?" No answer from this girl who is wearing pink boots.

Lina smooths down her hair again. She smiles at a nearby boy. She sits on her knees inching out of the corner. She comes closer to the teacher.

"What is it Lina?" Ms. Franklin asks.

"Daniel is making that swizzing noise again," she says, while looking at the boy.

"Lina can you face this way? Lina, what are we talking about? What are they drilling for?"

"What do you mean?" Lina asks.

"Are you listening to our conversation?" asks Ms. Franklin.

"Yes," she says.

Ms. Franklin turns away and calls on another boy. Lina moves her head from side to side then slides backwards into the corner again.

What does an identified non-school ready child look like? In what ways is he[1] perceived as non-school ready? And why do we, as early childhood educators, continually engage in the practice of sifting through children looking for what they are lacking and then classifying young children as being non-school ready?

In 2014, I conducted a qualitative research study on school readiness and how the non-school ready child is perceived/evaluated by the early childhood teacher. During this study, I observed five different low-income Black[2] children in kindergarten and first grades, and followed them around over a course of six months in order to understand how they were being documented as being non-school ready. I interviewed their teachers as well, and during this process I realized that the promotion of *school readiness* in actuality is a deficit construct that further marginalizes the so-called non-ready child and perpetuates discriminatory practices.

Lina, the only girl in the study, is identified within the first two weeks of school. She takes too long at finishing tasks, has trouble adapting to the rules of the classroom and is non-verbal. She is also African American, and her teacher is upset to hear that Lina's parents believe there is a "bit of a racial issue" involved in Ms. Franklin deciding to send Lina out of the room for academic intervention[3] services. The parents are worried that Lina will eventually be classified and placed in a special education environment. Ms. Franklin believes that special education testing may help clarify Lina's emerging academic issues. At the end of first grade, the parents refuse testing, and Ms. Franklin reluctantly promotes her to second grade. In most cases, however, the identified non-school ready child is referred to the team and is either removed from the regular education classroom or remains, but is pulled out for most of the school day for services.

An identified non-ready child, in most cases, is a non-White child from a low-income/working class background whose parents are working multiple jobs in order to survive. He derives from differing backgrounds (i.e., African American, Haitian, East African, Dominican and etc.) that are culturally out of sync with the normative early childhood program discourse based on White middle class values (Burman, 2007; Cannella, 1997; Lubeck, 2001; Randolph, 2013). The parents can lack the language background (English Language Learner) or concertive cultivation (Lareau, 2003) necessary to navigate the schooling process. In short, this child is outside the system even before he enters the system, and once inside is quickly identified as not fitting into the early childhood schooling structure. With the increase of higher standards, this child is failing before he starts. He is classified as non-school ready and is syphoned off to special education, retained or excluded from mainstream schooling.

We all embody different ideas about childhood that draw on a variety of circulating discourses that help us make meaning of *school readiness* in low-income Black children. My goal is to disrupt the everyday identification of *school readiness* (children who are labeled non-school ready) and question the ongoing usage of this term within the early childhood community. The term *school readiness* has a variety of similar definitions, but the one I am utilizing relates to "the preparedness of children to learn what school expects or wants them to learn" (Edwards, 1999, p. 1). Specifically, this refers to reading and literacy skills, math skills and the socio-emotional behavior of a child entering kindergarten or first grade. The expansion of this term includes how children fare at being able to adapt to this normative school culture. Lina, according to Ms. Franklin, has not adapted well to the culture of school. She is a good example of how a child who is identified as non-school ready functions or does not function well in an American public school.

School Readiness

School readiness, as a term, appears for the first time in the 1960s during the implementation of Head Start, a nationally funded preschool program designed for low-income urban young children. The founders of Head Start, including Zigler and Styfco (2010), utilize the term *school readiness* in order to justify the need for Head Start programs in poor urban areas. The program is designed to give low-income non-White families a 'head start' on formal schooling. Many longitudinal quantitative studies (Barnett & Boocock, 1998; Lara-Cinisomo et al., 2004; Zigler, 2006) over the last forty years have been conducted to prove that children who are classified as school ready fare better in later formal schooling. The belief is that by attending to the issue of *school readiness*, children fare better throughout their schooling careers and also have more success in the job market as adults. This application of *school readiness* is ironically utilized as an attempt to close the gap of inequalities in the early childhood schooling years.

School readiness refers to reading and literacy skills, math skills and the socio-emotional behavior of a child entering kindergarten or first grade. The teachers in this study expand this definition by including a myriad of social expectations. Examples of such social expectations of behavior include: children's ability to sit still, to listen, keep their hands to themselves, share materials, raise their hands and walk in a line. Since there are children who are unfamiliar with these cultural routines because they have not attended preschool, or have had limited preschool or subpar preschool experiences, there can be a culture clash when they first formally attend school. Numerous quantitative studies on *school readiness* (Barnett, 1998; Lara-Cinisomo et al., 2004; Magnuson et al., 2004; Rock & Stenner, 2006; Zigler & Styfco, 2010) conclude that there is a racial disparity in the *school readiness* skills of White middle class children and low-income Black children. According to Zigler, 35% of all entering kindergarten children are deficient in *school readiness* (Zigler, 2006; Zigler & Styfco, 2010). "If students enter kindergarten at a disadvantage, early gaps in understandings of literacy and math tend to be sustained or widened over time; this is particularly true for children of poverty" (Linder, Ramey & Zambak, 2013, p. 1). Therefore, *school readiness* is an issue for all populations, but is more acutely related to certain marginalized populations (low-income non-White populations) due to perceptions and assumptions of the dominant school and teacher culture that tend to be deficit-based.

Background of the Study

This book is based on my dissertation study of a narrative inquiry into how White middle class early childhood educators perceive or make assumptions when identifying *school readiness* in low-income Black children. This book differs from my dissertation because instead of focusing on how White middle class teachers perceive *school readiness* in young low-income Black children, it highlights the point of view of the young low-income Black child who is identified with this label. I believe this helps us, as early childhood educators, get a glimpse of what they struggle through on a daily basis.

The data collection includes an online district-wide survey of kindergarten and first grade teachers (n=24). Five of these early childhood educators (White and middle class) filled out the interest section on the survey and as such are identified as the participants of the study, which includes in-depth interviewing. I also observed the five different classrooms of each teacher participant I interviewed in order to follow one low-income Black child per class who has been identified as non-school ready. In addition, there are two different focus groups: one for the participant teachers (in Grayson School) (#1–5), and one designed as an interpretative focus group at a non-participant school in the same district with k/1 teachers (#6–11).

The study is conducted in a suburban/urban school district in the New York tri-state area with approximately 6,000 students in grades K–12. It is located within a few miles of a large metropolitan city, which has high populations of low-income Black children. Five elementary schools participated in this study, two of which are border schools with large populations of low-income Black children (55% and 35%, respectively). The former school that is the primary focus of this study is an elementary school that is located two blocks from the border of this large metropolitan city. I refer to this school as Grayson School. The five participating teachers in this study work in this one school. Two of them are multi-age teachers (grades 1 and 2), and the other three are kindergarten teachers. The identified non-school ready children in this study are respectively from each of their classrooms. The school's population consists of around five hundred students in grades K–5, one principal (Mr. Dodd) and one vice-principal (Mrs. Holland). It is housed in an old building (circa early 1900s). There are portable classrooms located in the back of the school near a large field with play equipment and a natural garden where the children grow vegetables. Behind the school there are low-income multi-family houses in poor condition. The neighborhood is a low-income Black area of town. None of the teachers, including those who reside in this town, live in this particular section of town.

Grayson is a designated Title One school, and 43% of the students qualify for free and reduced lunch, the highest percentage in the district. This figure would be much higher if White children did not opt-in. Many years ago this was a majority low-income Black school, and the district decided it needed to attract middle class White families from the other side of town. The district changed principals and the school's focus, transforming it into a school related to one theme.[4] The district now gives all families the option to choose Grayson. If they decide to attend, they are provided with free bus service to and from the school. Many White middle class families and a small number of Black middle class families who desire more diversity in their children's school population and are intrigued by this option (and the school's theme) opt-in. This has diversified the school to some extent, but during the past few years the percentages of opt-in children have decreased, as more families choose to send their children to their neighborhood schools instead. Tours of the school are conducted once a month by the principal for families in the district. If the families are interested in the school, they complete the necessary paperwork at the district office and apply for the free bus service. Some parents also drive across town to drop off and pick up their children, even though they live far enough away to receive the free bus service if they want it. The district is currently deciding whether to restructure the district or create a new theme for the school in order to continue to attract White middle class families so this school can continue to appear desegregated.

The Lens of the Study: Constructivist Grounded Theory

I utilize Constructivist Grounded Theory in this research study. Charmez's book, *Constructing Grounded Theory*, talks about constructions rather than discoveries, and how we, as researchers and people, make constructions based on our own preconceived ideas. This means that I have to be very aware of bringing my own assumptions and subjectivity into the research process. The whole purpose of the original Grounded Theory approach is to build theory from the ground up without personal bias influencing the data analysis (Strauss & Corbin, 1997). Categories and themes have to be constructed from the data itself and not from the researcher's own preconceived notions (Charmez, 2014). The Constructivist approach to Grounded Theory centers on a more reflective process.

Engaging in reflexivity is mandatory as a researcher, and even though I try to be reflexive in my research inquiry, I soon realized I harbor presumptions that are clouding my interpretation of the data. First of all, as I stated before, I needed to reflect on my own biases and assumptions, including issues related to race and class (MacNaughton, 2005). This research lens offers me a different perspective or view of myself as a researcher and brings key assumptions to the foreground. As I explain in the next section, during this process I have to come face to face with my own everyday pedagogical processes (i.e., referring too many Black children to special education testing). I critically challenged my own thinking on class and race during this research, which helps me to critically analyze a taken for granted practice.

Insider Status

As a White middle class early childhood educator myself, I have questioned my own attitudes and perceptions of a low-income Black child's *school readiness*. I have noticed in my own first grade classroom that children coming to school with no prekindergarten or limited day care experience do not fare as well during their first grade academic year. Interestingly, these children are predominantly low-income Black children. I began to question the term itself and wonder if my White middle class values based on the dominant discourse of schooling affected how I perceived and identified non-school ready children.

Furthermore, I began to notice that all of the children I refer to the child study team for special education testing are low-income Blacks. Actually, the highest referrers of Black children tend to be White teachers, sometimes at a rate of 30% to 50% of their classes (Harry & Klingner, 2006). In retrospect, I realize that I have neglected to refer several White middle class students who have exhibited reading issues in my classroom and are later diagnosed with learning disabilities. I am unconcerned about them at the time because of the ample support they receive at home. As a result, I unwittingly colluded with mainstream schooling practices and identified them as ready for school when they could have been perceived as non-school ready. Research, I decided, is the way for me to dig deeper into this issue in order to fully understand the scope of its magnitude of impact on low-income Black children.

One of the main reasons I decided to pursue this specific project is that as a first grade teacher I am interested in exploring how this observation, that more low-income Black children are classified as non-school ready, comes to be a phenomenon. I have spent my whole teaching career (fifteen years) in schools with large non-White populations, situated in low-income neighborhoods, and ended up at Grayson five years before this study. I am, just like my teacher participants, a White middle class female with preconceived ideas about what makes a child non-school ready. I could have been a participant in my own study.

There are some real positives to my insider research status. As a first grade teacher myself in the same learning environment, I can relate to the teachers' responses and have an understanding of the language they use. I feel comfortable with the teacher participants in my project, having known them to some degree beforehand. They, in turn, seem to feel comfortable with me and are very candid in their responses. There is a sense of camaraderie and mutual respect, and an interest in the subject of *school readiness*. The children (Derek, Lina, Michael, Billy and Jay) are also very friendly with me and know me from seeing me around Grayson. They seem to enjoy my visits and my time interacting or just observing them. My insider status also gives a firsthand view of one of these children (Jay) in my own first grade classroom. This gives me a more complex sense of him and helps me to better understand that these children are all individuals with individual needs.

During the interview process I observe the participants in their respective classrooms at different times and unofficially observe them outside on the playground and at lunch. Before I began this process, I asked each teacher participant to identify one low-income Black child in her class that she has previously classified as non-school ready. On my initial visit I locate this child and observe him or her and the teacher while taking field notes. The objective is to observe the identified non-school ready children in their inter-actions with the teachers and in how they participate in daily school life. I observe them for 20–40 minutes each at different times of the day. I take lengthy notes that I then expand into field notes (Emerson et al., 2011). As I compile the field notes later in the day, I include my thoughts on what trans-pired. These are reflections on the process, since I am not a neutral observer. "No field researcher can be completely neutral, detached observer, outside and independent of the observed phenomena" (Emerson et al., 2011). In the following days I write memos on each observation so that I can continually reflect on the research process.

Each teacher in this study (#1–5) selects the interest section of the survey, indicating that they want to be a part of the second research phase (includ-ing interviews, observations and a focus group). These teachers all work at the same school (Grayson) and I know them to varying degrees. They range in age from twenty-seven to fifty-four. They are the sole teachers in their respective classrooms, with twenty-two or twenty-three children per kinder-garten or first grade class (an average of fifteen of whom are Black children).

Introducing the Five Identified Non-School Ready Children

The five identified non-school ready children are central to this study and in turn are the key to the premise and understandings within this book. Each teacher participant is asked to identify one low-income Black child in her class whom they have classified as non-school ready at the beginning of the year to be a part of the study. This task is easy enough to consider, as all five teachers have large populations of low-income Black children (ranging from fifteen to seventeen children in their classes) to choose from. Ms. Moore only has to look at her coat rack (in order by arrival) and pick one of the five children who registered late for school (Derek). Ms. Springstein chooses one of her seven low achievers, and most active boy, whom she believes came to school non-school ready (Jay). Ms. Franklin selects her only clas-sified non-school ready child, who happens to be African American (Lina). Ms. Watson chooses from several different Black boys who receive support in her classroom (Michael). Ms. Smith picks the only boy who cries dur-ing the first week of first grade (Billy). These selections are teacher based and relate to their own criteria of what is considered school ready (see Chapter 3). It is important to note that not one teacher participant chal-lenges the direction of selecting a Black child. They do not even consider any White children who might fit this category, which is very telling in itself.

Lina

Lina from Ms. Franklin's class is the first child I observe. She's a first grader in a multi-age setting (grades 1/2 class). She is new to the school and did not attend a public school kindergarten. She attended the daycare where her mother worked until she started at Grayson. When I first meet Lina, I notice she chooses to sit closer to the teacher, usually near the front and off to the side. She seems very quiet and only speaks in whole class settings when spoken to, and even then only gives short responses. She's small in stature and her hair is tied up in a ponytail on most occasions. The first time I visit, she spends the whole period playing with her hair, taking it out and putting it back into her hair tie. Another time, I observe her return from AI (academic intervention), and she spends a few minutes alone behind the bookshelves by the coat rack before she is greeted by Ms. Franklin and asked to come join the class. Still another time, she reads her published book (from Writer's Workshop)[5] to the class, and half the class is not listening or positively responding to her story, whereas the girl who reads after her gets immediate applause when she is finished. I believe she's shy and has some trouble making friends. Other girls, some older and some the same age, sometimes boss her around and it's clear she does not like that. Ms. Franklin says Lina looks more like a kindergartner than a first grader. She immediately notices that Lina is not ready for school. Lina has trouble using the bathroom properly and sometimes has an accident in the classroom after returning from the bathroom. Ms. Franklin is very frustrated with Lina, which is clear when I observe them together for the first time.

Lina is behind academically. Ms. Franklin believes it has to do with her lack of kindergarten experience. She does not think very highly of Lina's experience at a daycare at her mother's job site (a large pharmaceutical company). Her mom brings in portfolios and shows them to Ms. Franklin and is later shocked to hear that Lina is so far behind academically.

The factors that relate to Lina's identification as non-school ready include: working too slowly, being non-verbal, not participating in whole class settings, not following class rules and lacking the ability to utilize the bathroom properly.

Jay

Jay, also small in stature, has long braided hair and smiles all the time. He seems very happy go-lucky and often laughs or jokes around with others. He likes to dance and enjoys all the songs the kindergarten class sings on a daily basis. He, too, prefers to use short responses and does not raise his hand, except during my last observation in June. He seems very well-liked, and as Ms. Springstein puts it, "is a good friend." He is eager to please and often approaches Ms. Springstein to show her what he is working on in class. He likes it when she gives him praise and works better with her nearby. It is important to note that Jay is in my first grade the year after this research study, and thus, I have a clearer sense of him.

According to Ms. Springstein, he jumps around and dances, and has trouble listening. In addition, he does not know how to cut with scissors, write his name smaller or properly handle a book. He works very slowly (which is a distinct non-school ready indicator). Ms. Springstein describes her concerns about Jay:

> He kind of goes with the flow. He just sits at his desk and continues to do it (cutting with scissors) . . . even when we are on the rug . . . and he knows . . . okay I am going to finish my work. Sometimes I just let it go and he does not have to finish it because I just want him to be a part of the group.

She worries about his slow work pace and his inability to finish his work. She also has concerns that he will be left out of the whole class discussion if he continues to work until he is finished.

Jay sits at a rectangular table designed to hold four children maximum, but there are six children at his table, so it is very crowded. His teacher states,

> It's tiny (the portable) and we can't fit . . . if you notice other portables have different tables. They have large flower tables, so they can fit six kids at a table. I have rectangular tables . . . that really can fit four to work comfortably. Everything is a logistical nightmare. I do rug writers (children who write at the rug) because there is no room to write at the tables.

As a child who loves sports and movement, Jay needs more space. The culture of rushing (see Chapter 3) is not conducive to the academic success of a child like Jay, who works at a slower pace. Ms. Springstein has to keep him on task so he can advance to the next task on time; otherwise he will always be behind. He also has trouble remembering class rules, like raising his hand.

Ms. Springstein is reading a book for mother's day.

It is called "Five Minutes of Peace," and is about a mom trying to get some alone time by taking a bath but her kids keep bothering her.

"What is the mom trying to do?" she asks in the middle.

"She wants to chillax. She wants to be in the shower all alone," Jay calls out. Everyone laughs. His teacher tries not to laugh and calls on someone else. Later on the boy in the book puts a bowl on his head.

"Spilled over!" he calls out again.

"What's pleasant mean?" she is ignoring him.

A girl states, "It's not good."

Jay is raising his hand in the air wildly.

"They are playing with food and not eating it," he shouts out before she has a chance to call on him.

"I am going to wait," she says and she stops reading.

He nods his head when she starts to read again. He is listening carefully.

"Will she ever get some peace?" she asks.

He shakes his head no and raises his hand again.

"What is the baby going to do?" she asks.

"Stick his head in the bathtub," he says after she calls on him.

"Will she be happy?" she asks. "Thumbs up or down."

Kids put their thumbs up and down in the air.

"I put a thumbs down," he says quietly to no one.

"So when you give your mom the teapot and poem for mother's day you are going to give her five minutes of peace," she says.

"I am going to break in," he calls out as he raises his hand.

Everyone laughs.

"Jay you are all up with your hand today," she says and he smiles.

The factors that relate to Jay's identification as non-school ready include: being too active in a small classroom space, not listening or following directions, not finishing his work on time, being needy and calling out.

Michael

Michael, who is also a kindergartner, is in Ms. Watson's class in a nearby portable that is a bit larger in size. He is tall and has short cropped hair. He is quiet and also only speaks when asked to participate. He's very comfortable in math and genuinely likes playing math games with others. He sits at the back of the rug at an assigned spot and is paired with the same boy during partnering sessions. He does not seem to need extra attention or approval from Ms. Watson. Instead, he seems to enjoy being left alone to attend to his work. Michael sits perfectly at the back of the rug listening to Ms. Watson's Writing Workshop mini-lesson. His hands are in his lap or on his chin. Ms. Watson says that he is "reluctant to raise his hand" and has a "strong hesitancy." She wants him to raise his hand of his own volition more frequently. She states that he is in the bottom third of her class, and that because he has been absent so often earlier in the year, he has slipped farther back and is less ready for school than he was at the beginning of the year. According to her, he has missed 24 out of 180 school days so far (in March). She feels that he is "more with it" when he attends school consistently. This reveals that the label of non-school ready is not necessarily a fixed one, as Michael had been considered school ready at the start of the academic year. His absences, however, contribute to his being labeled non-school ready by mid-year.

He is very good at math, so I am confused as to why she has classified Michael as non-school ready. Is it because he is too quiet? Or because he is absent too much? When I ask Ms. Watson why she identifies him as non-school ready, she admits that she has selected him because she knows the family and has taught the older brother, and therefore wants to help Michael succeed. She has concerns about his progress and feels strongly that his many absences affect his progress. In January, she notices that instead of writing a sentence he draws circles on his writing paper. She knows he can do better. "I think that after he has been absent for a while . . . he'll come back in and he'll lose motivation," she says, "and it's my job to get him back on track."

Even though Michael excels in math, he apparently has some issues with writing. He has not met the expectations of the teacher in this area and she worries about his progress. He also does not raise his hand often enough and is not vocal in the classroom. To some degree, Ms. Watson discounts Michael's abilities in math, which is interesting because research (Moses & Cobb, 2002) indicates that being good in math is a strong indicator of *school readiness*. In addition, math is an important civil right for Black children, as they need to understand it in order to contribute to society later on (Moses & Cobb, 2002). However, during our interviews she is more concerned about his lack of writing and reading skills.

Michael has his hands in his lap, then he puts his chin in his hands. He is sitting at the back of the rug listening to Ms. Watson's writing lesson.

"Now I have to think of a title," she says to the class. She holds her marker up in the air and pauses.

"Let me think," she says. Everyone is quiet, waiting. "What are my choices . . ." and she writes three possible titles of her made up story on experience chart paper.

1) My friend Donna
2) My first play-date
3) My crummy play-date

Out of nowhere she says, "Michael are you ready?" He sits taller.

"I think I want to choose this one . . . it is more mysterious," and she points to the third choice, My crummy play-date.

A girl raises her hand.

"They will look inside and they will be surprised," she says.

Then she models making the front cover—writing the title on the easel.

"How many pages across?" she asks suddenly.

Most of the children, including Michael, hold up three fingers.

"Michael I love how you are showing three fingers."

He does not react to her praise.

"We are going to return to our seats and come up with our own titles. . . . Are we going to draw a picture in the picture box?" she asks.

Children shake their heads.

"Michael?"

"No," he says firmly.

After they go to their tables Michael tries to get the student teacher's attention.

"I need help spelling Halloween," he says to her. His big brown eyes look up at her.

"Write what you hear," she says and then she is gone.

He writes it out saying each sound as he writes it The *hlloween nit*, he writes. He then writes his name in the author spot and starts to draw a picture in the box.

"NO DRAWING," Ms. Watson yells at his direction. And he drops his orange crayon.

Here, it is clear that Ms. Watson is frustrated with Michael even before the activity starts. She is a stickler for following directions and she knows Michael will have trouble following her instructions. It is very hard to give a kindergartner a sheet of paper with a box for drawing and tell them not to draw. Michael is not the only one in the classroom who wants to draw. During this time period I notice her yelling at a few girls for taking out their colored pencils.

As I re-read my field notes, I can't help but think that if Michael acts more verbal in class, perhaps he would not be classified as non-school ready. He seems quiet and soft- spoken, and does not raise his hand during any of my observations. Instead, Ms. Watson calls on him to answer her questions, which helps her to determine whether he truly understands the lesson. At one point in our discussion, she reveals to me that she is surprised by how much he raises his hand while I am in the room. She even discusses it with the student teacher and they both question whether he is doing it to show off in front of me. I, of course, refer back to my field notes, and notice that there are no notations to indicate that Michael ever raised his hand in my presence. When I mention this to Ms. Watson, she insists that he does raise his hand. I am sure Ms. Watson truly believes that Michael does take the verbal initiative because she wants so much for him to voluntarily be a part of the discussion. This is interesting because part of the school culture is raising one's hand, taking the initiative to say something and participating in discussions on one's own terms. Clearly, Ms. Watson and I differ in our perceptions of Michael's participation levels in class. Class participation is an important trait that is graded in kindergarten and appears on the report card. Shy or quiet children who do not take initiative, for whatever reason (e.g., cultural differences, personality differences), will not meet the school's expectations and will receive lower grades.

Despite demonstrating some key school readiness indicators, Ms. Watson still labels Michael as non-school ready. Furthermore, she believes that although Michael starts the year more school ready, his many absences cause him to fall behind. As a result, his status changes. This case reveals the arbitrary nature of *school readiness* identification.

The factors that relate to Michael's identification as non-school ready include: his lack of participation, his excessive absences from school and his reticence in whole class settings. The fact that Michael excels at math is not enough. He needs to excel in reading and writing, too. It is also interesting to note that Michael sits perfectly on the rug and at the table, which is another *school readiness* indicator presented by the participating teachers.

Derek

Derek, another kindergartner, is also tall with short hair. His first language is Creole, and his mother and other relatives speak only this language. He is tested for ELL (English Language Learner) and passes the test. He is supposed to go to the ELL program at another school in the district but is unable to attend because of a conflict with his mom's work schedule, as she can't pick him up from the bus. He likes having jobs in the classroom and responds well to being in charge of materials. He also needs to be near his teacher, whom he completely adores. He stands by her table or lingers nearby and waits for her to invite him to sit at her table. His assigned rug spot is directly in front of the teacher so she can physically reach down and touch him on the shoulder when he's distracted. He responds well to praise, like Jay and Billy (described below), and his face lights up when the teacher gives him put-ups. Like Jay and Billy, Derek is also highly active and constantly distracts himself.

Since Derek loves Ms. Moore, he gets upset when she gets mad at him. He wants her ongoing approval and attention all the time. She says that if he is able, he likes to sit by her all day long just to be near her. When he goes to the bathroom, she reminds him to turn off the water in the sink. When he comes out, she reminds him to fix his belt. He diligently pulls up his pants and returns to his seat.

Derek is Haitian and speaks Creole a lot in class. Ms. Moore says that he sometimes speaks Creole to other Haitians in the classroom, but stops whenever he sees Ms. Moore looking at him. He knows that her expectation is that he only speak English in school, so he tries hard to do that, yet sometimes it is just too tempting, as there are at least five other children in his class that are fluent in Creole too and he wants to interact with them in his home language.

Derek is exceedingly likable. He has a great working relationship with Ms. Moore, which helps his progress. He clearly needs to be physically near his teacher, but this is hard for her because she has a class of twenty-three kindergartners, all with different needs that warrant her attention.

It is quiet work time after lunch. Ms. Moore is at her desk. Derek is not at his table.

"Green table . . . uhhhhhhh (loud voice) stop and sit down."

Derek comes out of the bathroom inside the portable.

"Is there anyone else that would like to read me their work?" she asks the dark classroom. Derek skips toward his seat, but doesn't sit down. Instead he walks over to the teacher's desk and just stands next to it. Ms. Moore is talking to the boy at her desk. He doesn't seem to mind. She sees him after a moment.

"Why are you up again Derek? Go sit down."

He puts his head down and walks back to his seat.

When he sits down he swings his legs back and forth.

"Can I have hands and eyes!" she says suddenly.

"HANDS AND EYES!" they scream together.

She starts giving long directions and then stops herself.

"Whoa . . . that's a lot of directions," she says.

Derek gets up as others all move at once. He rotates to the next table and sits down. He is blocking a girl trying to move around him. The tables are too tight.

"Hey," says the girl.

"Excuse me," she says to Derek.

He gets up without a word and lets her pass.

"Derek why did you get up from your table? Go back to your table . . . take a chair from over there," she says loudly. He goes back to his table but does not sit in his seat. He sits at the head of the table instead.

Others continue to walk around as she gives directions.

"I see confusion. . . . Listen carefully. We are not walking from center to center."

Derek is trying to follow directions, but he is unsure of what to do. He needs to keep moving as he is a bodily kinesthetic learner and has trouble sitting still, so he moves around the room a lot. His teacher is frustrated by his movement and calls attention to it regularly.

The factors that relate to Derek's identification as non-school ready include: his inability to follow school culture, his difficulty working independently, his inability to adapt to routines and his surroundings, being non-verbal, distracting easily and being highly active.

Billy

Billy, like Lina and Jay, is small in stature for his age (first grade). He is in Ms. Smith's multi-age classroom (grades 1 and 2), and like Derek and Jay responds very well to praise from his teacher. At times he will approach her and ask if he is behaving or doing well. He also likes to show her his work on a regular basis and ask if he is doing it right. He, like the others, only responds when called upon, and until the very last observation does not raise his hand of his own accord. He is sometimes unfocused and has a tendency to distract himself with nearby objects. He calls out a lot and only stops when Ms. Smith ignores him. He works hard for a sparkle (an object she throws to a child who is working on task) and wants to please his teacher, but never seems to gets one.

The second time I enter Billy's class I have trouble locating him because the children are in different seats. He is very quiet, lying on the table with his head in his arms. He doesn't raise his hand either, a consistent theme with all five child participants. He looks up and listens but says nothing. On my last visit a month later, however, he is a different person. He raises his hand and calls out constantly. He seems more comfortable in the classroom space, but he is still having trouble following school rules. At one point, Ms. Smith reminds him that he is not asking a question but instead is making a comment, so she cuts off his narrative. Calling out (not being able to wait to speak) is another non-school ready indicator that these teachers cite. He also lacks control of his body. During one observation, I watch him remove his right shoe three times and wipe his foot with his hand. Later, when I report this to Ms. Smith, she says, "Oh, I didn't notice that . . . he's not usually." She later tells me that she has the ability to tune out things when it gets too hectic in her classroom.

Billy, who is just starting to participate, is still having trouble navigating the culture of the school (e.g., raising hands to speak, not calling out). He finally engages in the lesson, but is still unsure about how to do it. Ms. Smith praises him when he raises his hand and calls on him frequently, but she ignores him when he calls out to send him the message that calling out is not allowed.

Billy has his head on the table. It is Writing time and Ms. Smith is giving instructions.

"Hands on your head," she says. And some children put their hands on their heads. Billy doesn't move.

"We are going to be writing . . . finish a story . . . start a story," she instructs.

Billy is tapping the container of supplies in the middle of his table.

"Mirror me," she says. Everyone looks up.

"I," she says,

"I," says the class,

"will re-read,"

"will re-read,"

"my story,"

"my story."

Billy is not responding. She instructs everyone to get their writing folders. Children get up and move around. Billy falls out of his chair onto the floor. He crawls back to the chair and sits in it backwards.

"Blue table," she calls. He gets up and moves forward a few feet before he stops at the next table. There is a crowd by the shelf of writing folders. He tries to maneuver inside to grab his folder but a big girl pushes him back.

"Mine," she says to him.

He tries again to reach his folder. He finally gets his yellow folder and grabs a pencil.

"I am the third one," he says to no one. He touches his pages, flipping through them. He walks up to Ms. Smith.

"This is . . . this was in my thing," he says holding up stray pieces of paper.

"It's——(another boy's)," and she takes the pages from him.

He walks back to his table, can't find his writing sheets and walks back to his teacher.

"I looked and I still don't see it."

"You don't see it . . . look in your yellow folder," she responds.

He goes to his cubby and searches for his missing pages.

Everyone else is now settled at their table writing.

He walks around the room still looking.

Here, Billy is having trouble following directions. He falls out of his chair, which is not unusual, as active boys this age have trouble sitting in chairs. He also can't find his story. He is moving all around the classroom in search of missing pages.

The factors that relate to Billy's identification as non-school ready include: his inability to follow school culture (e.g., not being able to raise his hand without calling out), being non-verbal, being highly active, being needy/lacking independence and working too slowly.

All of these children are victims of a deficit construct. In this book the reader will engage with each child and visibly see what they endure on a daily basis within the confines of the American school system. Hopefully, identifying and understanding these five children thoroughly will fundamentally challenge how early childhood educators perceive *school readiness* identification/classification.

Making Dominant Practices Visible

This book's main job is to make dominant practices in early childhood education visible. The more visible these pedagogical practices are, the easier it is to critically reflect on them and call for a change in policy and practice. Visibility leads to change, and as such can make a difference in young low-income Black children's schooling.

In this case, *school readiness* identification is the taken for granted practice analyzed. This national discourse and practice is currently being touted as the best practice to follow. The Brigance,[6] Bataille[7] and other tests that measure four and five-year-olds before they enter kindergarten are supposed to tell us how the child will or will not fare in formal schooling. Teacher educators, policymakers, educational corporations and parents alike are promoting *school readiness* skills. Thousands of books are offered on Amazon that relate to getting children more ready for school. This is a complex industry/practice that must be questioned. Naming taken for granted practices, such as *school readiness*, is imperative at this stage in history, as noted in the next chapter, because a deficit-based historical practice cannot be interrupted until it is made transparent.

Furthermore, deficit thinking and related pedagogical practices will continue to be perpetuated in future policy forms unless interrupted. This further widens the educational gap between the White middle class young children and low-income Black young children. Breaking the deficit cycle is not an easy task, as it has been an integral part of the history of early childhood programs and how they operate. Martusewicz writes that "the effects of deficit thinking play the most important role in constructing perceptions of inferiority, creating a racist society" (Martusewicz et al., 2011, p. 157). Deficit constructs are racist constructs and as such need to be challenged.

School readiness represents the logic of domination related to White middle class values. Bell hooks states that "the politics of domination are often reproduced in the educational setting" (hooks, 1994, p. 39). According to hooks, transformative pedagogy that relates to the freedom to learn can't be achieved unless dominant practices that reproduce racist structures are challenged (hooks, 1994). Therefore, pedagogical practices that create or reproduce deficit constructs need to be examined and eradicated in order for true learning to take place within the school system. This book intends to critically challenge the dominant logic of *school readiness* and hopes that the reader will be a part of the movement for changing historically deficit and racist practices that affect the schooling of young low-income Black children.

Notes

1 I am utilizing 'he' when referring to non-school ready children because in reality more low-income Black boys are classified than girls.
2 I specifically chose to use the word Black instead of African American for two reasons. The first is that the Black children in Grayson come from a variety of Black populations (i.e., Haitian, East African, African American, West Indian and etc.). Secondly, this book is centered on issues of race and challenging racist ideologies, so utilizing Black, noting skin color, is paramount to this critique.
3 Academic Intervention is a pull out reading or math program—usually 30 minutes a day.
4 The specific theme can't be revealed, as it may somehow relate to the identification of this particular school.
5 Writer's workshop is based on the practices of Lucy Caulkins and Teachers College. It includes free writing of stories, independent practice and publishing of student work.
6 The Brigance is utilized in most states and is scored from 0 to 100 based on how children answer certain questions (i.e., naming parts of the body, colors and etc.). Children that score below 65 are of concern to the teachers in this district.
7 The Bataille is an assessment instrument that measures developmental milestones.

2 The Historical Context of the Non-School Ready Child

The historical context of school readiness as it relates to the promotion of deficit-based theory and practices is crucial to understanding how low-income Black children (such as Billy, Michael, Lina, Derek and Jay) are currently being identified as non-school ready at a higher rate. My contention is that the surrounding historical and theoretical discourse related to this topic perpetuates racism and deficit-based pedagogical practices in early childhood programs. In order to challenge this deficit-based term, we need to critically analyze the historical context and theoretical underpinnings that are attached to *school readiness* identification.

In this chapter I examine the recent history of American early childhood programs (from the early 1900s to the present day) and critically analyze how they specifically perpetuate deficit discourses related to low-income non-White populations. I explore the historical context of American early childhood programs and the rise of the term *school readiness* as a commonplace notion. I also unpack the relationship of early childhood education and its deficit context by reviewing the following: the theory of cultural deprivation, the anti-deficit ideology that critiques this theory and the rise of the standards and accountability movements, including the neoliberal school reform movement, that further shape this ideology.

Historically, early childhood education is in large part stigmatized as poverty-based programs intended to provide services that later increase productivity and economic prosperity in the United States (Beatty, 1995; Tager, 2015). The historical context surrounding early childhood programs *has not* been predicated on the natural rights of all young children to receive a fair and quality education (Roosevelt's radio address, 1930s). I contend that American early childhood programs have been designed to alleviate the stressors of poverty and change the moral attitudes of poor people instead of designed to address the educational needs of the families they serve, especially low-income non-White populations.

Furthermore, these early childhood programs identify impoverished young children and their families as somehow deficient and perpetuate the belief that these families do not value education. Immigrants and non-White families are blamed for their young children's lack of *school readiness*, and therefore White philanthropists have to step in to save them from their lack of 'moral upbringing.' As noted below, these programs are predicated on charity and the notion that these non-White low-income families lack the moral fiber necessary to be productive role models for their children.

The following historical early childhood programs are examined in order to challenge the deficit-based construct of *school readiness*: Day Nurseries of the early 1900s, ENS schools (Emergency Nursery Schools) of the 1930s, The War Nurseries of the 1940s and Head Start (1960s).

The Day Nursery

The Day Nursery movement of the early twentieth century was designed and implemented by middle and upper class White women. Day Nurseries are funded by philanthropic groups such as the New York Charity Organization and are developed out of a direct need to help immigrant and other classified non-White children out of the depths of poverty. Polakow refers to Day Nurseries as "a saving strategy—saving children from vice and saving poor defective mothers from abandoning their children and descending into the moral turpitude of prostitution" (Polakow, 2007, p. 5). Laura Spelman Rockefeller and Josephine Shaw Lowell worked to raise funds for these centers, which are located in the urban centers of America. Most Day Nurseries were open six days a week, twelve hours per day and took charge of children aged six weeks to six years old, much like day care centers today. These women "expressed great concern for the plight of small, dirty, ill-behaved, lower class children who were left alone daily, often tied to the bed post or to the casual oversight of neighbors or older siblings while their mothers went off to the factory or domestic work" (Steinfels, 1973, p. 41). The Day Nursery was seen as a temporary and emergency measure, because mothers were not supposed to work, and if they did work, they were expected to do so only for short periods of time until they could raise their families out of poverty.

Josephine Lowell Shaw, one of the leaders of this movement, believed in Social Darwinism and the notion of the survival of the fittest. According to Shaw, "the fit should be encouraged to have children, while the unfit should be prevented through coercive means necessary, from reproduction" (Waugh, 1997, p. 118). She referred to these poor non-White mothers as 'feeble-minded' and in need of saving, and she believed pauperism can be cured through individual discipline (Waugh, 1997). This is much like the meritocratic argument today utilized by teachers who think that hard work can overcome the stressors of poverty (see Chapter 6).

The depression of the economic markets in 1893 left millions out of work, and it was up to Shaw and other White middle and upper class reformers to assist in caring for these 'pauper' children (Waugh, 1997). Lowell blamed poor people for their 'weaknesses' and therefore felt obligated to help them.

Blaming the so-called victim of poverty re-emerges as a theme in the 1960s and still resonates today (see Chapter 5). Poverty, according to these philanthropists, was the result of behavioral failures and required treatment through charity. They believed that the moral adjustment of the 'pauper' child not only benefits that particular child or family but society at large. This was the primary goal of the Day Nursery movement.

Day Nurseries vs. the Nursery School

Nursery schools were also developed around this time and are not based on custodial care or poverty control. Instead, they're designed to meet the needs of the whole child and provide him or her with pedagogical exploration and opportunities. This program, led by the progressives, such as Margaret Naumburg, Caroline Pratt, Helen Pankhurst and Marietta Johnson, was based on Western developmental psychology and designed to provide learning through experience. These programs were either private (Little Red Schoolhouse, Walden School, etc.) or university lab schools (Bank Street, University of Chicago). In either case, these schools were only available for middle and upper class families due to hefty tuitions.

The economic segregation between Nursery schools and the Day Nurseries illustrates the historical inequity of the two-tiered preschool system in America that still exists today. Day Nurseries "were the embodiment of class stratification where upper class volunteers ran the board meetings and managed the nurseries allowing no input from matrons, staff or mothers" (Polakow, 2007, p. 5).

All the power and decision-making processes were in the hands of the wealthy fundraisers, like today (Grayson's PTO is run by White middle class families that are the minority of the school). The pedagogy of these centers is based on the dominant paradigm of a class-based society in which one class (the poor non-White immigrant) is inferior to the other. Day Nurseries are created to impose White middle and upper class values and philosophies of culture onto marginalized populations. The participants in this movement are excluded from the process itself. Their voices are not heard or deemed important in the functioning of these centers. (See Chapter 5 to see how this relates to Michael, Billy, Jay, Lina and Derek). On the other hand, the Nursery schools model progressive education within their own class boundaries and ironically espouse inclusive philosophies even though they do not cater to low-income families.

The pedagogy and curriculum differ as well, as the Day Nursery was designed to provide custodial care and does not necessarily intend to educate the young child. In contrast, the Nursery school employed a solid play-based curriculum and advocated for the exploration of materials and concepts in order for the child to increase his/her knowledge base (Beatty, 1995). This difference in pedagogy clearly illustrates the unequal education practices that filter down to the modern day two-tiered preschool system.

Emergency Nursery Schools

In the 1930s, the federal government, under the direction of President Roosevelt, recognized the need to help boost the struggling economy by sponsoring a variety of programs that provide temporary relief to workers. One such program was the ENS preschools (Emergency Nursery Schools). They offered jobs for teachers and helped families on relief with much needed childcare services.

In the first year, 2,972 preschools were established, primarily in conjunction with local public schools. By the second year, the program dropped to 1,900 schools (Beatty, 1995). The National Advisory Council of Emergency Nursery Schools formed in order to attempt to maintain overall quality in these schools. However, the temporary nature of these schools, and the high teacher turnover, made them more of a custodial care program than a true preschool program. The council soon realized that the quality of care was in question.

According to Mary Dabney Davis of the National Association for Nursery Education, the premise of the ENS preschools was "to provide an environment in which children for whom the school system is not yet responsible, children under five, would be so normal and happy that they shall be relieved of tensions of worry or despair which are found in many homes suffering from financial insecurity or overcrowding due to the depression" (Davis, 1933, p. 90). These preschools were just another emergency relief program designed to foster a stronger economy. They did not last.

The War Nurseries of the 1940s

During World War Two, the number of women who entered the workforce increased by 76% (Beatty, 1995). They primarily worked in wartime factories. It was then considered patriotic to serve your country by taking over a man's job on a temporary basis. In 1943, as a part of the Lanham Act, the federal government opened over 3,000 new preschools (Beatty, 1995). For the first time, even though it was temporary, the federal government advocated for a preschool curriculum that fosters educational growth in young children. Former ENS schools (that have remained opened) fell under the umbrella of the War Public Services Bureau. Unfortunately, the interest in developing and sustaining an actual preschool curriculum waned after the war ended, and the schools shut down.

Gender norms, at the time, dictated that women return to the home after the war in order to resume caretaking of their children. Therefore, it was no longer normal to be working outside the home, as women were considered the primary caretakers. Again, this established a deficit construct for these families, as children are supposed to be at home with their mother, and families where the women has to work were outside this norm. Thus, there was a stigma attached to this 'non-traditional' family. This remains especially true for single mothers of Black children (i.e., Billy and Derek).

Head Start (1960s)

Probably the most significant historical early childhood program is Head Start, which still exists today. In the 1960s, President Johnson declared a "War on Poverty"[1] and funded many social programs to counteract this American problem. With an initial budget of 50 million dollars, Head Start was born (Zigler & Styfco, 2010). The idea behind Head Start is to provide impoverished, mainly non-White children access to schooling and social welfare programs before the age of five so they are more ready for formal schooling. This program was designed to satisfy the complete needs of the preschooler and their families, including: parental workshops, health visits, dental exams, meetings with social workers and educational enrichment. Ironically, Head Start has never been funded through the Department of Education but remains (even fifty years later) under the Department of Health and Welfare. It is categorized as a War on Poverty program and not an educational program, even though it is touted as a model preschool program.

Head Start, much like the previous early childhood programs mentioned, is based on the notion that a specified population (non-White children) embodies a perceived deficit. These programs are based on the 'cultural deprivation theory' of outside dominant White populations (Ames & Ellsworth, 1997). The notions of cultural deprivation and the imposition of a White middle class value system on marginalized children are similar to the Day Nursery over 100 years before.

Furthermore, all of these above described historical programs emphasize a deficit-based model, as they are based on economics, naturalization, religion and other mainstream value systems, instead of educational pedagogy. These programs assume the low-income non-White populations they target suffer from cultural deficits. This historical context is indicated today in early childhood programs, as it continues to function in a two-tier system where either low-income non-White populations have no access (such as Billy and Michael) or limited access (Jay and Derek) to a quality preschool environment.

Theory of Cultural Deprivation

The theory of cultural deprivation is paramount when considering the historical context of the deficit-based practices of early childhood programs. The term itself gained prominence in the 1960s, and this theory relates to all of the early childhood programs described above. The term postulates that certain populations (low-income and non-White) are both environmentally and biologically deficient and therefore in need of extra support (Bloom, 1964, Bloom et al., 1965; Riessman, 1962). The term *school readiness* relates directly to this premise, as it is based on the supposed deficiencies that these populations have before they enter formal schooling. Therefore, these marginalized populations need *school readiness* skills (i.e., Head Start) in order to function effectively within the dominant school system.

The theory of cultural deprivation is based on the research findings of Bloom, Hunt, and Riessman. In 1965, Bloom listed over 116 empirical research studies as evidence of the existence and importance of this theory (Bloom et al., 1965). Examples of these research studies include: Empey (1956), whose findings concluded that low-income youth did not aspire to achieve, Vera's (1963) findings that low-income children were unable to think abstractly, Krugman's (1961) research that illustrates the effects of cultural deprivation on low test scores and Weaver's (1963) findings that 'negro' low-income children are deficient in auditory learning practices (as cited in Bloom et al., 1965). These studies, which may be considered racist and discriminatory today, emphasized the cumulative deficits of this population in the schooling process. They considered these deficits to be alienating and disruptive to the classroom and to their possible achievement.

At the same time, the Moynihan report, *The Negro Family: The case of national action,* surfaced and received critical attention. Moynihan believed that the Black family, itself, is a detriment to the quest for civil rights (Rainwater & Yancy, 1967). This report focused on the so-called deterioration of the Black family (e.g., the dissolution of marriages, illegitimate births, single mother households and increased Welfare dependency) (Moynihan, 1964). Moynihan and others (Bloom et al., 1965, Hunt, 1961; Moynihan, 1964; Riessman, 1962) specifically cited these Black families as culturally deprived due to the following factors: lack of a male figure in the household, lack of interest in the child's education, low educational levels of the parents, poverty and limited language skills (Bloom, 1964, Hunt, 1961; Moynihan, 1964; Riessman, 1962).

Anti-Deficit Theory

Scholars known as anti-deficit thinkers (Keddie, 1973; Labov, 1973; Pearl, 1997; Valencia, 2010) attacked the basic premise of the cultural deprivation model, which essentially blames the victims (low-income Black students) and their families for their perceived school failure (see Chapter 5). Valencia (1997, 2010) refers to the theory of cultural deprivation as a deficit model. He concludes that there are six basic characteristics of this model. It:

- Blames the victim,
- Is utilized as a form of oppression,
- Is based on pseudo-science research,
- Is a dynamic model that changes historically,
- Is utilized as a catch all or mode for the educability of a child,
- Is controversial by nature (Valencia, 2010).

According to him, this model remains continually in play, because it can explain the school failure of low-income Black children within the dominant school system. This directly relates to the five children in this study, as they are constantly being blamed for not being school ready, and so are their families. Furthermore, being identified as non-school ready is a form of oppression, as they are eventually weeded out of the mainstream classroom environment.

In his breakthrough book, Keddie (1973) compiled a variety of articles/ research from that time period that refuted the deficit model. Labov directly assaults the notion of 'negro' children as being verbally deprived. He contends that there is a great deal of verbal stimulation in their homes, but due to institutional racism, educational researchers and policymakers cannot comprehend the verbal acquisition or language differences (Labov, 1973). Lina is a good example of this, as she is considered verbally deprived by her teacher. Ms. Franklin is constantly prodding her to speak more, trying desperately to extend her verbal abilities, but Lina does not capitulate.

Postman, another anti-deficit scholar, centers his research on the 'political act of reading.' He believes that the American schools are "designed to produce one sort of human being rather than another" (Postman, 1973, p. 83). His research concludes that the educational system, itself, is responsible for the reproduction of certain types of values and beliefs (normative paradigm) and is never inclusive to marginalized populations (Postman, 1973).

Furthermore, Pearl (1997) and Ryan (1976) both conclude that blaming low-income Black students and their families is not the answer to the widening educational achievement gap. Ryan argues against the notion that any one group or family can be the problem. Rather, he places the entire blame squarely on the racist school system, citing school segregation, inequities of funding and lack of cultural insight on the part of the teachers in general. Pearl agrees with this contention and believes that the problem will continue to flourish and mature so long as educators and policymakers need a scapegoat to explain the ills of the public school system (Pearl, 1997). Thus, the five young low-income Black children in this study are scapegoats, as they are labeled as non-school ready and unable to achieve.

The High Stakes Testing Movement

According to Valencia and Solarzano (1997), the theory of cultural deprivation experienced resurgence during the 1990s, as educators and policymakers utilized 'at-risk' constructs and terminology to describe certain underperforming populations. The rise of high stakes testing inflamed the deficit model resurgence, as 'at-risk' students (generally low-income and non-White) were blamed for their lackluster scores. Valencia refers to this specifically as "a modern form of educational oppression" (Valencia, 1997, p. 5). There is no doubt that all five of the children in this study will be labeled 'at-risk' in later schooling years, as their test scores will fall below average. This contention is based on their inability to pass kindergarten and first grade assessments (see Chapter 4).

Furthermore, policies such as the NCLB (No Child Left Behind) and Race to the Top further this deficit approach. The NCLB, initiated under the Bush administration, is a policy that was designed to fail. By 2014, all children were expected to reach 100% proficiency in reading and math (Ravitch, 2010). This goal was unattainable from the start. It set schools up for failure and held teachers, children and administrators accountable for not measuring up. In Race to the Top, the allocation of federal funds is tied to these high standards, and therefore many school districts lose funding if they do poorly on these tests. Grayson school and their district lost federal funds from Race to the Top because the conservative governor did not apply for them in a timely manner, mainly because he's anti-public schools and wants them all to fail anyway.

Everyone loses—the teachers, the administrators and especially the 'deficit' children, who are now more visible and vulnerable and officially branded 'deficient' and 'at-risk' students (i.e., Jay, Lina, Derek, Michael and Billy). The 'at-risk' constructs are now replaced with terms such as 'not proficient' and 'not school ready.'

The Neoliberal Agenda

The term *school readiness* is a part of the present neoliberal discourse surrounding public schools in America. I am utilizing Harvey's definition of the term neoliberalism, as a theory of political economic practices that advances entrepreneurial freedoms (Harvey, 2005). His term 'accumulation by dispossession' refers to corporations making a profit while others do not. This is directly tied to the continual marginalization of specific populations, such as poor or low-income people (Harvey, 2005). The political economy of early childhood education programs in capitalistic America is based on the marketization of young children. In order for young children to succeed as adults in the free marketplace, they need to be school ready.

What kind of future does a designated non-school ready child have? In my interview with Michael's teacher, Ms. Watson, she makes it clear that there is a place for all children in this economy. There is a need for children to grow up and be workers in the community, and her thought is that service jobs, although not considered important, are key to her student's future.

Ms. Watson:	I think it's important that we have . . . we are producing students that come out of here . . . that are . . .
Me:	successful?
Ms. Watson:	that are successful . . . that they feel successful and they know that they are contributing to society in a good way . . . to themselves in a good way . . . um (pause).
Me:	that's what you are trying to do.

Ms. Watson: yeah . . . whatever that may be for them . . . you know what I mean . . . whatever that may be . . . they don't have to say well I am going to be a doctor . . . they can be . . . I dunno . . . a garbageman . . . as long as they have good values . . . there's a job for everyone . . . you know . . . it doesn't matter as long as they are good people . . . and I mean good . . . by productive and positive.

Clearly, Ms. Watson, a White middle class woman, believes in the reproduction of socio-economic class structures. Does she see Michael as a future garbageman? A janitor, perhaps? She does not have the expectation that he will be a doctor, even though he excels in math and science. This is a very revealing statement, and as such relates to how these identified non-school ready children are viewed in relation to how they will contribute to our economy.

Jay, for example, who has already been identified as non-school ready, will probably suffer the same fate of his father, who dropped out of school and struggled to find a salaried position. As a low-income Black boy with learning issues, he does not have much of a chance in succeeding in mainstream public schooling and graduating with a successful career.

Billy, as of this writing, has moved to two different districts since Grayson, as his family has to keep finding short-term housing and job solutions to make ends meet. Like other poor Black families, Billy will struggle to stay in one school and even finish school on time or at all. This will affect his place in the neoliberal world order and will contribute to the marginalization of these populations.

Human Capital Theory

According to Becker (1994), a member of the Chicago School of Economics and a key player in this neoliberal discourse, particular investments in humans, such as education, can lead to greater business returns (Becker, 1994). Thus, people are only as important to society as their contributions to our growing economy (Keeley, 2007; OCED, 2007; World Bank, 2003). Becker's empirical research reveals that people with a high school diploma generally earn more money and therefore contribute more (i.e., through taxes).

This approach to public schooling becomes more about what the child will contribute to the future economy, rather than the child learning for the sake of learning and developing important human relationships that can later contribute to the public good. Being competitive within the larger global economy and contributing back to the local economy (through paying taxes and labor) are more important than the individual child gaining knowledge about the world and developing agency in early childhood settings (Adair, 2014).

Thus, the term *school readiness* is an important part of this neoliberal discourse, because at a very young age children (such as Jay, Lina, Michael, Derek and Billy) can be classified as non-school ready and therefore not as important overall to the future of our economy. This deficit construct stays with the child as they get older and limits their educational potential.

The Commodification of Education

Education as a whole, in line with this neoliberal agenda, is now a part of the larger educational industry run by the private sector. Profit is generated through educational products and services that supposedly promote *school readiness* in young children. This makes *school readiness* big business. Private companies (e.g., Pearson, ABC Mouse, Kuman, Sylvan, Kaplan and etc.) actually earn huge quarterly profits by offering products and services geared to the non-school ready child. "Kaplan says revenue for its elementary school divisions have doubled since NCLB passed" (Meier et al., 2004, p. 87). It only follows that the recent adoption of the Common Core[2] standards allows private sector educational companies to continue to reap high profits. It is important to note here that these large educational corporations need the adoption of the Common Core, so they can gear programs to one main set of standards.

Kuman and other educational tutoring companies are making huge profits from this particular state's adaption of the Common Core. Teachers in Grayson refer identified non-school ready children to Kuman all the time. This tutoring program is costly and it mostly caters to low-income Black children who are not measuring up to the new higher standards. Families have to pay for an intake testing session and then have to commit to at least two times per week for a six-week block. Both Jay and Billy are referred to Kuman, but their parents cannot afford it, so they do not ultimately attend. Other families within the school go regularly to this nation-wide program, spending money they do not have, trying to get their child out of the deficit-based position of being labeled non-school ready. This particular program consists of hundreds of drill sheets that children spend hours completing after a long day at school. As a first grade teacher, I have not found these drill sheets to be particularly effective because they utilize the same style of learning (auditory/linguistic) over and over again. This method does not work well with visual learners like Jay or bodily kinesthetic learners like Billy and Derek.

There is a direct link between the recent implementation of the Common Core standards and the for-profit educational industry. These companies, such as Pearson and Kuman, need the alignment of standards nation-wide in order to profit from their programs. Also, as the standards and expectations increase (see Chapter 4), more children overall will be classified as non-school ready and below grade level.

In summary, the examination of the historical context of American early childhood programs demonstrates that the rise of the theory of cultural deprivation of low-income non-White populations and the history of high stakes testing/standards all impact how the young low-income Black child is classified as non-school ready. Negative and deficit-based perceptions of these children are already assumed before the White middle class educator assesses them. Furthermore, the context of the political economy of early childhood education is very important in relation to *school readiness*, as the neoliberal discourse perpetuates this deficit theme by only catering to school ready children who will contribute to our growing future economy. This discourse also promotes corporations making direct profits from their raised standards (Common Core), therefore blurring the lines between the public and private sector.

Children, such as the five children in this study, who are identified early on as non-school ready, therefore have too much to overcome in order to achieve in this type of political economy. Instead they will be relegated to low-level jobs and will not be major contributors to our future economy (contributing taxes). They are blamed for their poor test scores, and their families are considered culturally deprived. The policies that are ironically designed to help them (NCLB, Race to the Top) further exacerbate this deficit construct. They are classified as 'at-risk' and 'not proficient' and cannot measure up to increased standards and high stakes testing (see Chapter 4). Past research, whether considered racist or not, is not on their side and only points to them as being a part of the problem. Instead of blaming the racist dominant practice of the American school system, these researchers blame the victims and as such perpetuate an ongoing cycle of deficit-based constructs. Ultimately, *school readiness*, as a term, relates to this oppressive marginalization of certain non-White populations within the school system and must be challenged.

Notes

1 Sergeant Shriver, who convinced Lyndon Johnson to put money into this major problem in American Society, designed the "War on Poverty." Many programs were formed under this initiative, but very few remain today.
2 Common Core is a universal-based curriculum that aligns with the national standardized testing practices in the United States. It is adopted state by state, with the majority of the states practicing it.

3 The Ecology of School Readiness

The ecology of *school readiness* relates to how White middle class teachers perceive *school readiness* or non-school readiness in low-income Black children in their classrooms. It examines how children who do not necessarily understand the culture of the school (based on White middle class norms) can be labeled non-school ready when they exhibit certain attributes and behaviors. It further examines the expectations that lead to this early identification, usually made within the first month of school as districts now mandate the grouping of children into various categories (high, medium and low) through district-wide assessments in reading and math.

In this chapter, I carefully examine and analyze how White middle class early childhood educators go about identifying and classifying *school readiness* in children and their specific expectations based on district-wide mandates. I will further explore how the particular teachers in this study identify *school readiness* in individual children, specifically, in Billy, Michael, Jay, Lina and Derek.

Specific components and factors relate to this identification, such as: the ability to follow school culture, having the appropriate socio-emotional skills and being able to work on a task in a timely fashion. The following table reveals specific teacher expectations of readiness for entering kindergarten and first grade based on the teacher participants (1–11) and the survey respondents (n=24). (See Table 3.1: School Readiness Skills.) These particular expectations of skills that are needed to be school ready directly affect the teaching trajectory in their classrooms. For example, if a child has trouble calling out and interrupting all the time (like Billy and Jay), the teacher has trouble attending to the lesson and keeping it within certain time constraints. Therefore, a deficit of these *school readiness* skills leads to an immediate classification/identification of non-school readiness. Derek's teacher, Ms. Moore, even says, "You can tell on the first day who has had some schooling . . . you know, even if it is not a full day preschool." Jay's kindergarten teacher, Ms. Springstein, goes so far as to say, "You can tell when we bring them in for orientation and we bring them in for screenings (Brigance test) you can tell who can't even sit for a ten minute test." It is important to note, however, that children who have had full day preschool before entering can still be identified rather quickly as non-school ready.

Table 3.1 School Readiness Skills

Ms. Springstein: (Jay) K	*Ms. Franklin: (Lina) 1st*
Plays with others	Socially mature
Is a good friend	Gets along with others
Listens	Able to listen to story
Uses bathroom	Is potty trained
Able to share	Is read to every night at home
Is organized	Can talk about a story
Can dress self	Knows how to sit
Walks in a line	Can unpack/organized
Knows a few letters	Knows letter sounds
Follows directions	Can wait turn to speak
	Follows directions
Ms. Watson: (Michael) K	*Ms. Smith: (Billy) 1st*
Can share in groups	Socially mature
Can share in partnerships	Able to Listen
Listens	Knows books
Is potty trained	Can talk about books
Able to sit for a story	Is read to every night
Verbal	Can give a verbal opinion
Can sit	Sits well
Manages/controls body	Knows ABCs
Takes care of themselves	Understands culture of school
Gets in a line	Knows numbers 1–20
Knows upper and lowercase (ABC)	
Ms. Moore: (Derek) K	
Plays well with others	Can control body
Able to listen	Organizes belongings
Uses bathroom properly	Follows directions
Knows books	Knows ABCs
Can talk about books	Dresses self
Can talk to other children	
Sits well on carpet	

The Identification Process

Her first grade teacher immediately identifies Lina as being non-school ready. The first major indicator is that she has not attended a conventional public kindergarten but instead attended her mom's work preschool/kindergarten program. This is an immediate red flag to Ms. Franklin, and thus, according to her, Lina starts at a deficit as soon as she walks in the door of her classroom. The next indication, which affects her classification, is her inability to handle bathroom procedures. One day she gets so lost trying to find the girls bathroom (it is not on her classroom floor) that she returns to the classroom and then has an accident on the floor. When Ms. Franklin recalls this story, she makes it clear that Lina has several issues with controlling her bladder, which she feels is inappropriate for a first grader.

During the assessment period during the first 30 days of school, Lina scores low on both the reading and math assessments. Her reading is designated as the beginning of kindergarten (DRA testing)[1] and her math skills are also below grade level, as she does poorly on the standard base line quiz. Ms. Franklin has to report all of her scores to the main office and reading specialists. Thus, within three weeks of school, Lina is already on the list for academic intervention, which means a reading specialist will pick her up daily to work with her in small groups. She also has an intervention meeting scheduled for her parents and the administrators, in order to work on giving her the most academic support possible.

Billy, Jay and Derek are all identified rather quickly because of behavior issues. They lack overall stamina, have trouble sitting on the rug and at the tables and score low on one-on-one testing because of their active body movement. These attributes/behaviors are more noticeable to teachers and therefore can be identified within the first few days of school.

Billy, who has no prior schooling experience, fails both the reading and math assessments. He is flagged early as a candidate for intervention and a meeting is scheduled with the vice principal, his teacher and his parents. He is also pulled out immediately for academic intervention and is referred to a school social worker.

Derek is classified as non-school ready during his kindergarten entrance test (utilizing the Brigance) a few days after school starts and receives a score of 46 out of a possible 100. The teacher immediately realizes that he may be an ELL candidate, as he speaks fluently in Creole, and tries to get him tested for the ELL program at another school in the district. He is not tested until late October, and by then he's already very attached to his new teacher. He passes the ELL test and is considered eligible for the program, but his mother is not able to get off of work to pick him up from the bus at the earlier time, so she keeps him in his kindergarten placement at Grayson.

Ms. Springstein states that "every day is an example of how Jay is non-school ready." The very day of this teacher interview, she refers to a moment that characterizes this behavior.

> We were sitting in our circle and we were doing our greeting . . . responsive classroom.[2] We do a share and then we do our morning greeting. This morning we did a greeting where I have all their pictures in a basket in the middle of the circle and their names written on the pictures . . . to help them. It is more for the beginning of the year to correlate the name with the faces. The child goes over to the basket, picks a picture and

says 'good morning' and they would high five each other . . . okay . . . walk back to your seat and sit criss cross applesauce and wait for the others. He (Jay) throws it into the basket . . . runs across the room and slides into his seat . . . like not even realizing the other kids around him.

Here, Jay lacks control of his body by sliding into his seat, and his teacher feels he has trouble listening and following simple instructions as well. He also exhibits focus issues and is reading below benchmark levels.

Michael is not identified right away, and is the exception to the others in this regard. "This child came in ready . . . appearing to be ready . . . to some degree," says Ms. Watson. She only becomes concerned in the middle of the year when he is absent a lot and misses important material covered in the classroom. She states that his academic abilities seem to have regressed in the middle of the year. She is especially concerned with his writing.

> He was just . . . he was just doing circles on his paper. . . . In Writer's workshop rather than drawing a picture about his idea or . . . he wouldn't even just illustrate his idea . . . and he disengaged with all the other children . . . even if they didn't have preschool . . . were doing something . . . even if they were stick figures . . . the child who I described (Michael) was having trouble just putting together his ideas . . .

Her concerns, she feels, are related to his increased absences. His father (and she makes a point to say that all the children in the family have different fathers) is not around much and his mom has to do most of the work herself. She thinks sometimes if the mom doesn't have work it is just easier to keep Michael home. Ms. Watson does not believe that the mom is doing any reading or writing at home.

Ms. Watson feels that Michael can also be silly sometimes with his friends and get distracted, so she carefully pairs him up with children who are on task. She is fearful that he will become a behavior problem. (See Chapter 6, which deals with race and the problems in discipline of Black boys.) She feels that by missing so many days of school, he is less motivated to do well or behave properly when he returns. She thinks it is her job to get him back on track so that he can be more successful in the classroom. To her, the absences lead to distraction and silly behavior in class. They are the real reason she considers him non-school ready. The following is an interview with Ms. Watson concerning Michael:

Ms. Watson:	I think that after he has been absent for a while . . . he'll come back in and he'll lose motivation.
Me:	Right.
Ms. Watson:	And it is my job to get him back on track . . . because it's easy for him to not be motivated.
Me:	Well, does he like school?

Ms. Watson:	I think he loves being part of this classroom community . . . I think he likes to learn new things . . . I think sometimes . . . the application part of it . . . he can be a self-starter but if he is being silly with someone else . . . or if he has been out of school . . . it can distract him.
Me:	Do you think that he doesn't like being out of school? Does he ever tell you how he feels about being absent?
Ms. Watson:	No . . . again . . . that's a part of the mystery because . . . (name of sibling) was an open book . . . where he . . . it's almost like he doesn't want to say anything against . . .
Me:	his family?
Ms. Watson:	against his family . . . I think he knows he shouldn't be out of school . . . that's why he is obviously making up excuses about it.
Me:	Okay . . . well if he is saying he is sick . . .
Ms. Watson:	right and he's not . . . and he's bowling (she laughs).

This exchange, like many others between us, centers on Ms. Watson's negative ideas related to being absent too much in kindergarten. She feels that his absences are not for valid reasons and that this directly affects his classwork when he returns. I have to wonder, however, if Michael came in every day on a regular basis, would he receive this classification of being non-school ready at all?

The Ability to Follow School Culture

The ability to follow school culture, based on the practices of White middle class norms, is imperative to the classification of school readiness. Ms. Smith refers to this as the ability of a child "to understand how a classroom is run." Following school culture means that the child knows what is expected of him and is able to follow these guidelines without being redirected. Ms. Smith and the other teachers in the study equate knowing and understanding school culture with being school ready. She states:

> They (school ready children) understand the school community and the school responsibility . . . like for themselves. They know and I am not talking about organization . . . but they know . . . they understand little things . . . like their homework folder . . . where they put their homework . . . that they have homework every night . . . and they may just throw all of their stuff in their book bags. But they understand what they need to do.

Ms. Smith highlights the main premise of school culture, which is knowing how to 'do school.' This point was important to all of the teachers in this study, because even though they realize that as an early childhood educator they must teach aspects of how to do school, they still want children to arrive having some knowledge of school culture and how it effectively works.

Jay's teacher, Ms. Springstein, a former preschool teacher herself, believes that learning how to do school and following school culture should be part of a preschool program, so that children are ready to enter formal schooling. To her *school readiness* includes being able to be a good considerate friend, work cooperatively, raise one's hand, walk in a line, and listen and follow directions. "I want my kids to do school so they are ready for school," she says in one interview. In other words, the prior school experience of children entering kindergarten is of extreme importance because that is where they should have been exposed to the culture of school. It is important to note the paradox of this statement, as children need school experience in order to be school ready, yet when they come to school for the first time, they are often identified as non-school ready.

In reality, however, first grade is the first mandated grade of education for children who live in this particular state. This varies state to state, some being kindergarten, first or even second grade. Here children are not required to attend school before the age of six. Preschool and kindergarten are optional in this state, and are not necessarily a part of every child's experience, especially low-income children. During this research process, there is only one public preschool classroom in the district, and it is limited to already classified special education students. Families must pay out of pocket to send their children to preschool, and it can be very expensive for a quality educational experience.

Since children are not mandated to attend kindergarten, Lina is able to stay at her mom's work place daycare. Her parents are pleased to have her there for as long as they can because her mom is nearby and can visit her on breaks. She's also able to care for her if she gets sick and does not have to worry about travel time to school to pick her up. It's a convenient situation that works well for this family. Both parents are very satisfied with the daycare experience and initially are shocked when Ms. Franklin relays her concerns. They present her with a portfolio of Lina's work showing how well she did in her old school, which does not impress Ms. Franklin, since it's not in a conventional kindergarten.

Derek and Jay both attend neighborhood storefront preschools, which do not prepare them as well for a traditional kindergarten classroom. Jay's preschool, *Learn to go to school* (changed only slightly in name), actually has not helped him 'learn to go to school.' They are not introduced to the culture of school, because they are in all Black preschool/daycares that do not abide by this normative school culture. Instead of learning to raise their hand, they call out to get the teacher's attention. They shout and use outdoor voices instead of quiet indoor voices. They watch videos and play outside. They do not practice lining up or sitting still in their seats. Some of the teachers in this study refer to these preschools/daycares as inferior to traditional preschools (that cost more money), but they are just following a different school culture.

On the other hand, Michael and Billy have no prior schooling experience. Billy spends his first week of first grade hiding under the table because he is so scared. School itself is a new experience for him and he doesn't like all of the noise and crowds in and out of his new classroom. It takes him a while to actually participate at all, and according to Ms. Smith, he is very young and immature in his behavior. Michael fares better without prior schooling because he is in kindergarten, not first grade, and he has an older sibling, so he has some idea of what to expect. He stays under the radar for the first month or so and then reveals himself to be a fair, if not average, student. They both, however, come into formal school at an extreme disadvantage, as they have no prior schooling and therefore have little to no exposure to the culture of school.

The ability to conform to the existing school culture is key to an incoming student. Clearly prior exposure to this particular school culture is helpful, which all of these children lack. Conforming is a way to stay under the radar, to not be classified or identified as being different, and low-income Black children have a harder time at conforming to this new culture. For example, in school it is expected that parents read to their children nightly. This is in line with the culture of the school. Yet, low-income non-White students don't always practice this cultural expectation and therefore are deemed behind in terms of school culture. As a result of not being able to adapt to this new culture (school), the child and their family are relegated to outside this culture. This furthers the educational gap between those who can conform or are a part of the school culture (White middle class children) and those who can't (low-income non-White children). This will be discussed at length in Chapter Five, as it deals with the differing cultural expectations between these children's families and the school itself.

Socio-Emotional Skills Needed

According to the teacher participants, in order to be able to follow school culture and be able to 'do school' properly, children need to be socially mature. This term relates to Western child development and therefore is defined by age range expectations. In his book, *Yardsticks: Children in the classroom ages 4–14,* Wood specifically defines what is considered socially mature for a child according to expectations of their age range. This is a standard reference guide that many early childhood educators utilize in order to gage whether a child is on par for his age range. Wood cites Erikson, a fundamentally important Western child psychologist, who gives specific guidelines for emotional/social development. An example of this is within Erikson's renowned psychosocial stages of human development. In the fourth stage, Industry vs. Inferiority (ages 5–12), he refers to children being able to actively be independent with confidence. Children that feel inferior within this stage (all five children in this study) are considered deficient in some way within the dominant Western socio-emotional standards (Erikson, 1950; Woods, 2007).

It must be noted, as will be explained later on, that this Western perspective of child development is not necessarily relatable to all cultures, which means that this definition of 'socially mature' may not relate to the local context of each child in this study.

What does socially mature actually look like in a classroom? It means that a young child needs to be able to play well with others, cooperate in groups, be a good friend, share materials, be organized, be kind and a thoughtful listener and follow the rules. These abilities are all indicators of school readiness for these teachers. Children who are not able to do these things are classified as non-school ready. They must be able to follow the culture of the school and provide the necessary socio-emotional skills needed to do so.

Interestingly enough, throughout this district the teachers cite socio-emotional skills as more important than academic skills in an incoming student. In the interpretative focus group, these teachers (#6–11) highlight this as essential to the learning trajectory of a child. #6, a kindergarten teacher, states:

> I think when you are talking about early childhood you are talking about it (socio-emotional skills) first because without these things . . . the academics can't come if the kid is not ready to receive it . . . socially, emotionally and developmentally.

They all agree that it is more important to teach social emotional skills before and during the process of any academic subject. To them, and the other participating teachers, if the child comes into school lacking in this area, it greatly affects how they do in school. Thus, if children come to school (K or 1) with varying degrees of socio-emotional skills, the academic gap widens over time within the school, and without these skills, they flounder grade to grade.

Jay is totally disorganized. His book bag is a mess and he can never find a pencil. Derek's seat organizer is so disorganized that it routinely falls down and explodes onto the floor when he searches for something. Billy also can never find his writing folder or the story pages he is working on. Lina is never ready to go to academic intervention because she can't find the book she is reading. These are some examples of how disorganization, as classified by teachers, can impede the academic process of a young child.

Lina also has trouble working with others. She sits alone a lot and complains that other children never offer to help her. On one occasion she is supposed to be working with her assigned oldster (a second grader), but she walks away from her because she says, "she wasn't helping me anyway." Ms. Franklin is frustrated by Lina's lack of effort in socializing with others and feels that this proves that she is emotionally immature and not ready for first grade. Lina, according to Ms. Franklin (as with Jay, Billy and Derek), is considered emotionally immature. She talks 'baby talk' and has lower level vocabulary. She utilizes words such as 'potty' instead of toilet and has trouble speaking in clear full sentences. She also lacks self-confidence, which Ms. Franklin relates to being socially immature. She speaks in a soft voice in front of the whole class and tries to hide on the rug in the corner so she is not called upon. She is also very needy, according to Ms. Franklin, and needs a lot of one-on-one attention. All of these are signs for teachers that she lacks socio-emotional skills.

Since Billy cried and hid under the table the first week of school, Ms. Smith immediately labels him as lacking the necessary socio-emotional skills needed for first grade. Like Ms. Franklin, she finds Billy very needy, constantly vying for her full attention. In a class of twenty-three children, she cannot give him all of the attention he needs during the day, which leads him to act out more often. She has a behavior system in place called 'sparkle.' When a student raises their hand, is listening and showing that they are school ready, they receive a sparkle. Ms. Smith throws the child in question a small sparkly ball and announces to the class that this person is sparkling in her classroom. I never once observe Billy getting a sparkle. He tries hard at times, but cannot completely contain himself, especially since he is in constant need of her praise. He approaches her regularly during the day to seek her approval on his work. Sometimes he gets instant gratification, and other times he has to wait a while just to get her full attention.

Ms. Moore also classifies Derek as lacking socio-emotional skills. His rug spot is directly in front of her because he is so needy that he needs to be physically near her all day long. "He likes to stand by my desk most of the day," says Ms. Moore. Wherever she is in the room, he's always nearby. It is clear to her that he functions better when she is physically near, so she adapts her seating arrangements to accommodate him. He is sometimes sitting at her desk even when she is working with another child. At one point I observe him approach her after using the bathroom and she just buckles his belt and pulls up his pants as if she has to do this on a regular basis. It must be noted here that Derek is one of the chronologically older children in his class. This is one of the reasons that Ms. Moore believes he should be exhibiting more improved socio-emotional skills. However, he just turned six and he is code switching all day long, trying to translate an English only class into Creole in his head. This takes a lot of effort and may affect the progress in his socio-emotional skills.

Today, the class is sitting in a circle on the rug while Ms. Moore reads the classic, *Make Way for Ducklings*. (This is a long book.)

Derek sits right in front of her feet, about a foot from her shoe.

"All of these horrid things," she reads. "What do you think horrid means?" she asks the class.

"Terrible," says a girl in the back.

Derek is whispering to the girl next to him who is ignoring him. He lightly touches her shoe. He is not looking at the book. Everyone is super quiet.

"I have seen the same hands for the whole story," says Ms. Moore, suddenly. "I would like some different hands."

Derek looks up and then looks away. He starts to play with his shoelace. He taps his shoe with his hand.

"Derek, can you remind me what ducklings are?" she asks him.

"Baby chicks?" he asks, unsure.

"Baby ducks," she corrects him.

A few minutes later, she stops and leans in to him.

"Drop the shoelace, turn around and put your hands in your lap." He does this right away.

He looks up. He looks down. His hands are now folded and he is trying to sit perfectly. After two minutes he jerks his shoulders up a few times, but his hands are still folded in his lap.

All of a sudden Ms. Moore turns to Derek.

"Derek what did she teach him?"

"How to swim," he responds quickly. And he is right.

He scratches his head and rubs his nose, trying not to move so much in his seat.

Here, Derek is trying very hard to follow directions and sit quietly. He has trouble sitting quietly as he needs to move his body and since the book is very long (seventeen minutes), he is having an extra hard time sitting still.

Socio-emotional skills are perhaps even more important to the teachers in the study because without them they find it hard to cover all of the material they have to cover in a six-hour day. Sitting and working well with others are necessary for them to rush through the curriculum without stopping for various behavior issues.

The Time Bind: The Culture of Rushing

A huge factor in the identification process of *school readiness* relates to the increased time bind in the classroom. Instruction time is highly constrained now due to the increased expectations of the Common Core and therefore directly affects a child who can't keep up with the advanced pace of the classroom. The challenge of time and the overall culture of rushing affects the daily routines of the teacher, because they must cover more material in a six-hour day. This, in turn, impacts the identification of the non-school ready child because all children must move forward at the same time even if they are not ready.

Harvey (1989) refers to increased time constraints as time-space compression. His research reveals that this is a direct result of advances in technology within economies, which include increased production speeds. Cultural changes can alter the relationship of space and time (Harvey, 1989). He states,

> We have been experiencing, these last two decades, an intense phase of time-space compression that has had a disorientating and disruptive impact upon political-economic practices, the balance of class power as well as upon cultural and social life.
>
> (Harvey, 1989, p. 284)

Schools too, are affected by this time-space compression, because they are a large part of our cultural and social lives. Therefore, the need to speed up and implement more instructional time highly impacts the identified non-school ready child.

Children like Jay, who work more slowly, do not fare well in this increased time bind. One of Ms. Springstein's biggest complaints is that Jay works too slowly. She sometimes lets him finish an art project before she beckons him to join the rest of the class, but he is never finished on time. Lina also works slowly. She always needs more time. Ms. Franklin usually calls her name before starting the next lesson. "Come to the rug, Lina . . . come now," she says. Lina tries to move faster but usually leaves her work unfinished on the table as she scrambles to catch up.

There is no time to waste in the modern American classroom. Instructional minutes are the most important minutes. Transitions, unpacking, packing up, snack and other key times in the day are not as important, and therefore the teacher is constantly rushing through them to get in more instructional time. In this particular school, the teacher is mandated to create a workable schedule that is approved by the principal and on file in the main office. Teachers at Grayson complain that they have to essentially create two different schedules, one for the main office and one real one, because they are not allowed to put non-instructional time on their schedules.

Teachers in this district are required to teach a certain amount of minutes for each core subject daily (ninety minutes of math, ninety minutes of reading/writing, thirty minutes of social studies and thirty minutes of science. There is a fifty-minute special, fifty-minute lunch and fifteen minutes for morning announcements, which all add up to six hours, with no minutes to spare). It should be noted that 6 hours is the contractual time of school in this district. Thus, there is no time for anything else. (See Table 3.2 for Jay's kindergarten schedule.)

This is a culture of rushing. Children are rushing from one subject to the next with little non-instructional or down time in between. In Grayson, these five young children only have twenty-five minutes for lunch and twenty-five minutes for outdoor recess, which includes line-up time and being walked back to their classroom. Most children at five and six years old have trouble eating in such a short period of time and don't even have time to complete their lunch. Jay never finishes his lunch. He brings his

Table 3.2 Jay's Kindergarten Schedule

Breakfast
Unpack
Morning Announcements (school wide)
HW Review
Morning Circle (Calendar)
Reading Workshop
Academic Intervention
Writing Workshop
Special (Gym/Library/Art/Music/Computer lab)—once a week
Social Studies or Science
Lunch
Recess
Math and Math Games
HW
Pack Up
Dismissal

lunch daily and usually only gets to eat one or two small items in his lunch bag. Since his lunch period is the last one of the day at 1:25pm, he's hungry all day. There is also no daily snack time, because Ms. Springstein has cut it from her tight schedule.

Transitions are also a problem. Since teachers have restricted minutes per subject, if they go over the minutes for one, they are behind in their whole schedule. Moving from one area of the room to the other can take up valuable time, and teachers have no time to waste, so children are constantly being rushed to transition to the new subject in a different area of the room. Going from the tables to the rug, including cleaning up and putting papers away, can take time, and when a child works slowly, they can't make up that time. Thus, they end up coming late to the new subject and miss valuable information. This means they are always behind and are trying to play catch up, while leaving a lot of unfinished work on their tables.

Time limitations are not just in the daily schedule. Teachers have to cover more curriculum than ever before and therefore run into time constraints consistently. For example, many years ago in this district, there used to be three writing units in kindergarten and first grade classrooms, whereas presently there are seven units taught in the space of the same year. Increased curriculum demands (see next chapter) directly affect the time–space compression, and are detrimental to students that are having trouble keeping pace. Perhaps if Michael were a kindergartner five years ago, he would not have as much trouble keeping up in his writing as he does now, as he is expected to write seven different books (at least one for each writing unit) instead of three. Why does he need to produce more? Production has now become an important part of the school curriculum. Learn more, produce more and do it in less or equal time. It is as if the school is now a factory, in which the floor managers are speeding up production and making their employees produce at least twice as much in less time.

This is the essence of global capitalization, and in this case the school district (like the factory manager) is squeezing more out of its working teachers. The district expects more in less time. Devault states, "The new economy is bringing new stresses to working life. Many jobs are changing and mostly not for the better"(Devault, 2008, p. 25). According to Devault, there is a climate of pressure in which workers (in this case teachers) are asked to do more with less (cover more work in less time). This climate of pressure directly impacts the children in these new time pressurized class-rooms, as they are under the gun to learn more in less time.

Time, therefore, is out of the teacher's control, and as such, out of the students' control. Pacing can't be altered to the child's needs, but instead must be efficiently utilized for instructional purposes. In this new culture of rushing, the identified non-school ready child is judged daily. He is working too slowly. They are not up to par, and even with prodding and pushing, they always fall behind. It is a lose-lose situation for these children. And it has nothing to do with brainpower or their creative or academic abilities. It has to do with time and the ability to conform to the time constraints of the modern American early childhood classroom.

Time Management and Control Tools

Time limitations call for proper time management on the part of early child-hood educators and are also a huge factor in the identification of non-school ready children. Teachers therefore must keep the class on task through different techniques in order to conserve time. Every minute counts. During my observations, I notice that the teachers utilize varying management techniques or control tools, including: flickering the lights, hitting wind chimes, singing songs, clapping in patterns and more. In one observation, I note that Ms. Wilson utilizes nine control tools in a twenty-five minute period.

"Bum, bada, bum, bum," she calls out, and the class responds with "bum, bum." Michael sits up taller, as does the others. A few minutes later, still on the rug, she says, "MAGIC SNAP" and everyone snaps their fingers and sits up even taller. Michael has not lost focus at all, but seems used to the constant interruption of management tools. Ms. Watson is teaching a writing lesson, a subject she feels Michael is having trouble with, and everyone is on the rug. After the Magic snap she praises the class,

"Love it," she says. And almost immediately she says, "Ta Ta ___."

This tool is directed to a specific person, and when they hear their name after Ta Ta, they know they need to pay attention. She goes on to model what a front cover looks like.

"Remember, the title is what you want to share with the world."

Everyone just stares at her. Michael is sitting perfectly on his rug spot, waiting.

"How many pages are across your book?" she asks suddenly. Everyone, including Michael is holding up 3 fingers.

"Michael, I love how you are showing 3 fingers."

"Now turn and talk to your partner—talk about three possible titles and choose one."

He turns to face the same boy, the boy he always sits next to at the back of the rug. They whisper quietly and then turn back around to face Ms. Watson, a signal to tell her they are ready. She walks around and stops at them.

"You both have titles?" she asks. They nod their heads.

"Three?" she prods.

They turn and whisper again. As the boy talks Michael holds up a finger.

"That's one," he says. And he counts until the boy has three and then it is his turn. He is talking too low, I can barely hear him, but the boy next to him has more than three fingers up in the air.

"Bum bada bum bum," she says suddenly.

"Bum, bum," they shout back.

"Touch your nose if you have a title ready!"

Michael touches his nose.

"Touch your knee if you are still thinking of a title!"

His partner quickly touches his knee.

"I think we need one more magic snap," she says, although they are all sitting perfectly following her directions.

"1,2,3 Magic snap," and everyone snaps their fingers.

A boy is then called to the easel to share his possible three titles for his story. Michael sits quietly and is not raising his hand to participate.

Nine control tools in a twenty-five-minute period are a lot for any kindergartner to respond to, but especially for a child who is identified as non-school ready. Ironically, she is using them to keep all children on task, including the struggling child, and yet they seem so overwhelmed with all the interruptions.

Another issue related to the increase in time management control tools is that it cuts down on movement time or time to take a break from the intense workload. This means that bodily kinesthetic learners, such as Billy, Jay and Derek, have less time to utilize body movement in the classroom and are expected to sit for longer stretches of time.

Jay takes his own movement breaks, much to the chagrin of Ms. Springstein, but he needs the physical movement and the space to escape the time management control tools.

"Look at me," he shouts, during writing.

"I am dancing."

Almost immediately after she sees him dancing by his table, she rings the bell. Now he must stop dancing and put his hands in the air. Even though his hands are responding, his torso is still moving. This is Jay's method of handling all the control tools.

To another boy, Ms. Springstein says, "I am wondering why you do not have your hands in the air. I will ring the bell again and we will clean up and meet at the rug."

A few minutes later Jay is dancing by the rug.

"Janet, look at this," he calls to a girl sitting on the rug. And he dances for her, smiling his goofy smile. Ms. Springstein is in another part of the room yelling at another boy, so she doesn't see Jay dancing.

Now Ms. Springstein is clapping.

"To the rug," she calls out.

Jay now plops on the rug. His movement break is over.

In Derek's kindergarten portable, Ms. Moore uses control tools to foster quiet. It is clear when I visit that she does not like a noisy classroom. The lights are off and it is a designated work quiet time.

There is a sudden wind chime sound. She is tapping a silver wind chime that hangs above her desk. They freeze in their centers.

"I see confusion. . . . Listen carefully. . . . We are not walking from center to center." She says firmly. Derek is frozen by his math center, yet he had been moving from table to table prior to her wind chime sound. Derek is snapping rubber bands at his table. Four other children are there working with geo-boards, making shapes with rubber bands. He is making a diamond, and then a square, but his leg shakes as he stands at his table. He looks like he wants to sprint around the room. He needs a movement break. He taps his Air Jordan sneakers on the floor. He rubs the back of his head.

All of a sudden, I hear Ms. Moore yell, "DEREK _____!" She screams his whole name.

"I don't like what I just saw!" He looks up slowly and makes a sad face. He snaps a rubber band across the table.

He wants to be the rubber band. He needs to move.

Expectations of readiness include the ability to follow school culture, the ability to use the socio-emotional skills necessary for the school culture, but this all needs to be accomplished in a specific time bind. In order for early childhood educators to meet all of the new and higher demands, they must implement more control tools and foster a culture of rushing. All of this expedites the school readiness assessment of each child, and ultimately furthers the gap between the 'non-school ready' child and the 'school-ready child.'

In conclusion, there are many factors to being labeled non-school ready, including; working slowly, not being able to follow school culture, being socially immature or lacking in socio-emotional skills and more. The increased pressure on teachers to include more academic instructional time during the day directly affects the 'non-ready' child in a negative manner.

Rushing through activities has become the norm, and these five children are leaving a lot of work unfinished. They also do not have the physical space to move around and therefore take their own movement breaks, much to the chagrin of the teacher. Jay would dance all day long if his teacher would let him, and Derek needs to be able to physically move when he is exploring materials. Clearly, these five young children are not able to follow the culture of school, the paradigm of White middle class schooling. They call out instead of raising their hands, or they don't raise their hands at all, and they are unable to sit quietly (except Michael) and have a need to move around constantly. Derek and Jay have trouble organizing their book bags or their seat bags. Billy loses his writing work, and Lina can't find anything, including her homework.

Time control tools are more readily implemented so the teacher does not waste any instructional time. There is more overt pressure on the teacher, an expectation to do more with less time, and with the Common Core (as discussed in the next chapter), the demands are so pressurized that the teacher has no choice but to pass this pressure onto their students. This is a no-win situation, for the teacher and especially for these five identified non-school ready children.

Notes

1 Developmental Reading Assessments—these are tests that determine the grade level of the child's reading abilities.
2 Responsive classroom is a widely used behavior-based program.

4 Higher Demands
Putting Pressure on the Identified Non-School Ready Child

Higher demands on teachers directly affect the classification/identification of non-school ready children. Increased pressure to teach more and the expectation to get young children ready for state-wide testing impacts all children, but specifically affects low-income Black children, like Lina, Jay, Derek, Billy and Michael, who are then further excluded from the main-stream classroom.

In this chapter I unpack and examine the higher demands from this particular district, which trickle down from the state, that are placed on early childhood educators and analyze how these demands and web of expectations negatively impact the identification of school readiness or lack of school readiness in low-income Black populations.

The Common Core

These higher demands are directly related to the implementation of the Common Core, which is now the educational standard in forty-three of the fifty states. Governors, policymakers and corporate educators have created these higher standards, and early childhood educators have not been asked to be involved in the process. The Common Core is designed to ensure that the standards for learning in K–12 are consistent from state to state. The premise of the Common Core is that every student will be exposed to the same educational standard and curriculum, thus ensuring equal access to education throughout the United States. As a result, regardless of where a child resides, they will be exposed to the same quality educational content. This thinking, however, is flawed for many reasons.

First of all, who is deciding these educational standards? Early childhood educators have not been consulted or even asked to contribute their valuable knowledge of young children and how they learn. This would make a huge difference, as teachers with experience know what is instructionally appropriate for young children. For instance, they understand that teaching three writing units as opposed to seven gives a child more chance of success.

It is also important to note that since each state has differing laws, including differences in educational spending and use of property taxes, it is impossible to have these standards implemented equally state by state. Each state spends different amounts of money on each child's education. For example, Massachusetts spends $14,285 per pupil, but Oklahoma only spends $7,631 per pupil (NCES—National Center for Educational Statistics). This is revealing in itself, because Massachusetts is consistently ranked number one in educational quality, whereas Oklahoma is ranked at the bottom. This ultimately means that some school districts have more money to spend, while students in states that allocate less money per pupil suffer inequities that affect educational quality. Furthermore, property taxes vary from state to state (New Jersey and California are ranked the highest) and district to district. Since the taxes are tied to funding of states' school systems, they greatly impact the amount of money schools receive to invest in resources to aid in their new curriculum goals as related to the Common Core. Property taxes also pay teachers' salaries, which results in widespread discrepancies between salaries from state to state and district to district. Thus, as it stands now, each state and the districts within the state are trying to meet the Common Core standards with wide variations of funding. Clearly, some states will be more successful in achieving the new curricular standards than others.

Pushing Down the Curriculum

Another issue with the Common Core is that it invariably pushes down the curriculum by adding more assessments and higher-level benchmarks in earlier grades. Therefore, first graders are now given second grade work, and kindergartners are expected to learn first grade material. Billy's teacher, Ms. Smith states:

> You know kindergarten is not kindergarten anymore. There are no more nap times . . . there are no more half days. It's almost like kindergarten is the new first grade and first grade is the new second grade . . . and that's how I look at things.

It should be noted here that in this particular school district, kindergarten has moved from a half-day program to a full-day program because of higher demands/expectations coming down from the district. With the implementation of the Common Core, over three years ago, the schools have had no choice but to push the curriculum down, so that material originally covered in first grade is now covered in kindergarten.

Jay's teacher, Ms. Springstein, believes that this increase in rigor is harmful to the young child.

> We used to have Guided Reading[1] in January and now they (the district) want us to start in October and it is really not appropriate for kindergarten.

Ms. Springstein's concerns are legitimate. She knows that establishing reading groups (by reading levels) so early in the year, when most five-year-olds are not sure of their letter sounds, is a recipe for disaster. Young children who are not necessarily ready for reading can flounder when trying to decode words. She and other kindergarten teachers must give a reading assessment (in this case DRA) to a young child in the first two weeks of school and record their level. They must be at a certain level to be on grade level, and if not are flagged right away as being below grade level.

This is problematic because the standards have raised the acceptable grade level scores in line with the Common Core, which means that most children fail their first reading test upon entry. In my first year as a first grade teacher at Grayson, the DRA benchmark standard for a child at the beginning of the year was at a level 3 or 4. During my last year (six years later) the child has to come in at a level 6 or 8. (See Table 4.1 for DRA Benchmarks then and now.) This is a huge jump in reading level expectations, and therefore more than half of my class is identified as below grade level in September of first grade. The Common Core raises all reading and math benchmarks, which ultimately leads to higher classifications of 'non-school ready' children.

Jay is reading below grade level and has been all year. Ms. Springstein tells the father that she may retain him because of his scores. If Jay had been attending Grayson just a few years earlier, he would be cited as being on grade level in reading. But since the implementation of higher standards, he is floundering in kindergarten. At the end of the year, he is reading on a 3 DRA level, which as I earlier stated, would be exactly on grade level years before, but now is considered below grade level. She looks at his progress throughout the year, however, instead of relying just on the scores, and promotes him to first grade. She is nervous about this because she knows he will be classified as a low reader in first grade, but she hopes with continued intervention and possible special education testing (she believes he is qualified), his reading will improve. Another kindergarten teacher could have easily retained him, citing his low reading scores.

Lina is having trouble with her reading as well. Her fluency or lack of fluency is an issue. Ms. Franklin is frustrated by her inability to read aloud

Table 4.1 DRA Scores Then and Now: First Grade

Old Benchmark *(Before 2013–14)*	*New Benchmark* *(Since 2013–14)*
September—level 3	level 6
November—level 4	level 8
January—level 8	level 12
March—level 10	level 14
June—level 14	level 18

in small groups. She is below grade level in reading and needs to raise her DRA scores by the end of the year significantly.

Today in Writer's Workshop they are practicing reading their stories aloud. In a few days, Ms. Franklin is hosting a Writer's Tea and parents are invited, but Lina's won't be there since they work during the day.

"Lina, do you want to go first?" Ms. Franklin asks.

Lina nods her head yes.

"Lina goes first . . . reading for fluency," she says to everyone sitting on the rug.

"Be a good audience. Please sit on your bottoms . . . criss cross applesauce."

Lina goes to the front of the rug and sits shyly on the large blue cushioned rocking chair. It looks as if it swallows her whole. She starts to read but her voice is too low.

"LOUD . . . LOUD!" shouts Ms. Franklin at her.

"I already heard that one," a girl calls out.

Lina continues to read quietly. It is hard to hear her.

"How can you say it sound more scary," interrupts Ms. Franklin. Lina is reading with little expression.

Lina reads the line again with more expression. A boy makes a scary sound.

"Better," says Ms. Franklin.

"He . . . went . . . to . . . see . . . what's . . . wrong," reads Lina. She is reading very slowly.

"Oh, wait a minute," she says to Lina, "better with HELP, HELP!!!" She is still working on Lina's expression.

A boy and a girl are talking at the back of the rug.

"Shh!" says the teacher. She puts her finger to her lips.

When she is done reading, Ms. Franklin says, "Next time practice reading dialogue better, good job!"

No one claps. Lina gets up and sits down next to Ms. Franklin on the rug.

Ms. Franklin wants Lina to use more expression and read with more fluency. Her reading is choppy and lacks confidence at this time. The other children are not even interested in her story and do not clap for her, even though they clap for the person who reads right after her. Here, Lina is publically humiliated by being forced to read a certain way in front of the entire class. This will only hurt her confidence in this area and make her more self-conscious when she reads aloud.

With the increase in reading benchmarks and the pushing down of the curriculum, more and more low-income Black children will be classified as non-school ready. White middle class children fare better within this framework. This is primarily because White middle class children usually come to school at a higher reading level. They usually have a plethora of books in the house, and are exposed to reading in general at an earlier age. It also must be noted that because of the two-tiered preschool system, they have a more quality preschool experience. Therefore, when they enter kindergarten and first grade, they are usually reading well above grade level. Now, of course, with the pushing down of the curriculum and the increased expectations in reading levels, they are not doing as well as before, but they are still average or above average (exceptions are children with reading disabilities). This leads to many awkward meetings with White middle class parents that are surprised their child is not reading better. The teacher has to explain to anxious parents that the reading standards have increased and therefore their reading level (for example a level 6) is no longer above average. However, they are still not readily classified as non-school ready because they have met the standards.

Increased Assessments

Increased standards mean increased assessments. As soon as the young American child enters the door of kindergarten or first grade, they are bombarded by written tests.

In Grayson, each child takes four different reading assessments, two major math assessments, a pre- and post-assessment for each chapter of math (all year long), a phonics assessment, a computer assessment in math after each level, two different writing assessments and more. (See Table 4.2 for a list of assessments in first grade). These are just the mandated tests, as each teacher may give their own assessments as well.

In first grade math, there are nineteen chapters, and each child is required to take the pre-test and post-test for each, which adds up to thirty-eight

Table 4.2 List of Assessments in First Grade (2015) (Grayson)

1) Math chapter pre-test (19x per year)
2) Math chapter post-test (19x per year)
3) Baseline math test—3x per year
4) Baseline DRA (reading) test—4x per year
5) Phonics test
6) Rhyming words match quiz
7) Science assessment sheets—4x per year
8) Social studies assessment sheets—4x per year
9) Syllables quiz
10) Dictation testing—2x per year
11) Spelling tests—weekly
12) Writing assessment—2x per year
13) Computer math assessments—4x per year

*This list only includes mandated district tests and does not include any other tests given by individual teachers.

different written assessments per child. This does not include the two main math tests that are given at the beginning and the end of the year, to assess progress in the child and to officially score the teacher. Teachers in Grayson have to fulfill their SGOs[2] by the end of the year. This means that they utilize the data from the first math test in September to categorize the children in their class into groups of low, medium and high. All five children in this study are placed in the low range. Then they have to utilize specific benchmarks (given by the district) for each child. At the end of the year, they give the same math test and record the data. If the child meets the specific benchmark listed in the teacher's SGOs, then the teacher achieves their goals. If the child falls short of the promised benchmark, then the teacher's score goes down. This affects their overall rating at the end of the year (see section on teacher accountability).

From the young child's point of view, it is test after test. They are doing whole class testing and individual testing. And they are doing it all the time. Teachers at Grayson have a hard time scheduling in all the testing, because it takes up so much time. As a result they do it all day long. During math centers children are called to the teacher's desk for quick assessments. Reading specialists are also taking them out of the room. On average, a young child in this school is taking several different tests a week throughout the year, with even higher levels of testing in the beginning and the end of the year.

Children are even taking assessments when they are supposed to be playing math games on the computer.

Today, Jay is on the rug with an ipad. The lights are off and all the children are spread out around the room working on ST MATH. Jay is tapping lightly on the screen, he is looking down and seems to know what he is doing.

Every once in a while he jerks his head and counts aloud.

"Hey Ms. S. I am doing a tally," he calls out to his teacher.

She immediately starts to sing a song and everyone stops and sings along.

"Mark down a tally

Put it in a row

Mark down a tally

Put it in a row

Fifth one goes across."

She walks over to Jay.

"Jay let me see that," she says to him. He shows her his ipad.

"Oh you did it . . . good job," she says. He smiles brightly.

His cheeks are big and fleshy for his small head.

Jay is now rocking back and forth. He puts his tablet down again suddenly.

"I am never going to get to 100." He looks down sadly.

A nearby girl moves closer to him to help.

Jay is having fun playing ST MATH[3] until he realizes, once again, he can't get to the next level. He is doing the work, and even his teacher is proud of his accomplishments, but he can't pass the computer assessment and get to 100. What Jay doesn't know is that his teacher is digitally keeping track of his progress in ST MATH. She reports his scores twice a year to his parents and is constantly checking on his level of achievement. Meanwhile, Jay thinks it is just a fun math activity and not an assessment.

Ms. Springstein and Ms. Moore both complain about the seventy-five indicators on the kindergarten report card. There are just too many assessments involved with such a high amount of indicators. To these teachers, this report card is developmentally inappropriate and not a valid measurement of a five or six-year-old. When discussing this topic, Ms. Moore states:

> It's too much! I even think in November . . .the report cards are too much. I just think it's inappropriate . . . it's not appropriate . . . it's not appropriate! They are not ready. They are just not ready to come and sit at a table one-on-one. You can see them . . . looking around . . . am I done yet, so I can go back?

Ms. Moore is referring to the multitude of assessments that the kindergarten teachers need to give each individual student so they can rate the child a 1, 2 or 3[4] on the report card. She believes that the children are not even ready to focus fully on the assessments themselves, as they are still acclimating to school and the long full-day of kindergarten.

Each teacher is required to complete a report card and a personal narrative (based on assessment results) three times per year. Most teachers in this study feel overwhelmed by the sheer amount of data they have to collect on each child and are more interested in how the child progresses over the year.

Non-school ready identified children receive 1s and 2s on their report cards. All of the 1s indicate that he/she has not met the standards. The teacher has to make specific notes on these 1s and 2s and give suggestions to the parents of what to work on at home. At the parent teacher conference, they have to specifically relay their concerns about the child's academic progress and then they give the parents a heavy load of extra work for them to go over at home. Sometimes they are asked to find an outside tutor as well. Since the majority of these parents are non-White and working class, this becomes a heavy burden. They already overwhelmed by work (sometimes two and three different shifts/jobs a day) and do not have the time or energy to sit with their child to teach them skills they are lacking in school (see Chapter 5). Furthermore, there may be cultural differences in expectations, and as such, the parents don't understand why the teacher is not doing the extra work themselves in school. Teachers are then required to (based on these increased assessments) write in clear and plain language that this particular identified non-school ready child is in danger of being retained and not being promoted to the next consecutive grade.

It must be noted here that the teachers in this study also feel the pressure to score these children on the low side to cover themselves later on. Many teachers in the next grade will go directly to them to complain about 3s on report cards when the child is (in their eyes) clearly struggling. This of course is all very subjective. Some scores, in math and reading, are clear-cut, they either pass or do not pass, and therefore have a corresponding grade. However, there are many subjective areas that the teacher has to create their own rubric or just give a score based on their own observations, which can be biased and deficit-based. For example, there is a whole category on the report card that is called 'Habits for Success,' which are basically behavioral assessments. This is one of the main areas that identified non-school ready children do poorly on, because they are deemed to lack socio-emotional skills. A child in this case could get a 2 or 3 in other subjects but because of behavioral issues can receive many 1s in this particular section. This is a very biased section and is based on specific cultural expectations (White middle class school culture). Jay receives 1s in *ability to control tone and volume of their voice* and *the ability to control and manage his body*. The indicators themselves are culturally inappropriate to all cultures outside the normative discourse. In Jay's house, he is not taught to control the tone or volume of his voice, and as previously stated, he also attended a preschool that encouraged children to speak loudly.

Furthermore, it must be noted that these assessments/indicators are all socio-culturally inappropriate in the context of the local community. Grayson is located in an all Black community that encompasses many different cultures that are outside the norms of the White middle class culture of the school system. According to Cowie and Carr, assessment should be grounded in a community of practice (Cowie & Carr, 2004). The local community should be a part of all assessments young children encounter. Parents should contribute their observations and notes to the overall portfolio of the child, and children should be evaluated holistically, through their cultural background and specific learning styles (Cowie & Carr, 2004).

An example of this socio-cultural assessment is practiced in New Zealand in the Te Wharki preschools. The Te Wharki curriculum is an innovative bicultural curriculum that celebrates the local culture of the child. It provides a framework in which indigenous voices have a central place and are valued (Lee et al., 2013). Since there is a co-construction of a curriculum, there is also a co-constructed assessment process that is culturally sensitive to the young child. The strong connection with the local culture and families enables this to happen. This, however, is not the case in most American schools, where local culture is neglected and undervalued.

Developmentally Appropriate Practices

According to the teachers in this study, the higher standards and increase of expectations directly correlate to the engagement of developmentally inappropriate practices. This means that Jay, Lina, Derek, Billy and Michael are not experiencing enough developmentally appropriate tasks during the day.

As a term, developmentally appropriate practices (DAP) are a creation of NAEYC[5] and are considered a universal standard in early childhood education. These principles and guidelines are based on fundamental values that are deeply rooted in the knowledge of Western child development (Bredekamp & Copple, 1997). The main goal of DAP is to provide developmentally appropriate socio-emotional, cognitive and physical practices for teachers in early childhood education, so that there is a uniform standard for quality early childhood programs. These practices are based on Western developmental psychological practices (such as Erikson and Piaget), which for many years have been considered part of the normative discourse in early childhood education.

Teacher participant #6 states:

> You know as the academic standards have become more rigorous and demanding the developmental needs have been squashed to the side . . . from birth to age six the development is like no other in a person's life . . . it's now being condensed and squashed and four-year-old brains are still four-year-old brains.

This educator makes it clear that the increase of demands by the district and the state are a problem in the consideration of the developmental needs of young children. Free play, with child agency, and participation in developmentally appropriate activities (i.e., playing with blocks, creating a puppet show, playing in the kitchen area, etc.) are appropriate for these children and as such should not be excluded from the curriculum. A first grade inclusion teacher states:

> I think in kindergarten you should be learning through play. You should have a kitchen area, a block area. . . . A little writing station that has crayons and stamps. . . . It should not be where little people . . . five-year-olds . . . are sitting and holding pencils. There bodies should be moving. It's not a developmentally appropriate curriculum anymore. Kids are not learning through play. Kids are learning by sitting down and listening to the teacher talk.

It is important to emphasize that the teachers in this study believe that free play and the development of social skills are essential and developmentally appropriate. They may believe in this theoretically, but their actual practice is limited now due to the new and increased demands of the curriculum.

It is essential to acknowledge here that there is some controversy attached to the idea of developmentally appropriate practices as currently prescribed in their various mission statements. These particular practices are solely based on dominant discourses, specifically Western child development. Thus, the DAP (1997, 2009) are a part of the dominant discourse in early childhood education and reflect the present culture of early childhood institutions. Discourses are never neutral and instead can define and shape existing culture (Allen, 2008). Therefore, the written text of these position statements perpetuates an already existing ideology of the culture of the schools, a Western middle class normative discourse. "DAP is not based on what we think might be true or what we want to believe about young children. DAP practice is informed by what we know from theory and literature about how young children develop and learn" (NAEYC, 2009, p. 9). Within the DAP, it continually refers to the premise of Western developmental psychology as the only possible ideology to utilize/practice with young children. This does not take into account other practices/cultures that may be more reflective of local indigenous populations. It professes that these developmentally appropriate practices are based on the legitimacy of modern science and as such can't be refuted (Penn, 2008). This leaves no room for other cultural perspectives on child development.

In my interview with Ms. Watson, Michael's teacher, she utilizes this notion of a Western perspective on what is developmentally appropriate when speaking about Michael. The following is an excerpt from our conversation on *school readiness*:

Ms. W: Potty training and not just pointing to what you want . . . and saying can I have a tissue . . . rather than just tissue.

Me: Verbally able to express it.

Ms. W: Exactly . . . like they need to be able to articulate their wants and needs.

Me: Well . . . they need to conform to the culture of the school . . . is what you said before.

Ms. W: So culture of the school . . . School Readiness?

Me: Right.

Ms. W: What 's the difference?

Me: I am asking you.

Ms. W: I think to do school.

Me: It's about your perceptions.

Ms. W: Well school readiness though . . . so you think there is a public school out there that will allow children to not be potty trained?

Me: No I am not saying that . . .

Ms. W: Okay . . . that's school . . . that's a part of school culture. I think that is a given.

Me: I am not saying that. I am saying that there are different value systems.

Ms. W: Right.

Me: So it is hard to say . . . they should be following these value systems . . . if they are following other value systems.

Ms. W: Yes, I understand your point . . . your point is taken . . . but when you say school readiness . . . school readiness is being potty trained . . . school readiness is being able to . . .

Me: Well this is your perception of school readiness . . .

Ms. W: . . . as school readiness there's any teacher that has been told that we accept someone in diapers . . . like I don't think it's my perception. I think it's . . . I dunno . . .

Me: You mean in this particular case . . . there are rules . . . you have to be potty trained . . . is that what you are saying?

Ms. W: Yeah.

Me: They have different rules in different schools at different ages.

Ms. W: I have 'Yardsticks' right over there (a Western developmental psychology text). I am sure that has something . . . you know a red flag should be flown if (walks over to shelf to get the book) if someone is coming in . . . like I read literature on it . . . each age (walking back) (reads title to me).

Me: So those are developmental milestones?

Ms. W: Exactly.

Me: Well wait . . . because this is interesting . . . so you are following developmental milestones that are Western based and are based on middle class value systems.

Ms. W: And this is highlighted like you would not believe . . .

Me: I understand . . . but what I am trying to say is that we are asking them to conform to our system of beliefs . . .

Ms. W: Right.

Me: for school readiness . . . so they may have different systems. . . . That may be in conflict with our systems . . .

Ms. W: Perhaps . . . sure . . . absolutely.

Me: Because this book is based on Western thinking . . . perpetuating Western cultural ideas . . . so are we as teachers trying to get them to conform to our culture?

Ms. W: Yes.

This exchange reveals the problem with White middle class teachers following the protocols of Western developmental psychology and utilizing it as a basis for evaluating and measuring children from other cultures. Ms. Watson is proud to have this popular Western developmental psychology text, and she refers to it in order to see who is and who is not developmentally on target. In other conversations she makes it clear that she is unhappy with all of Michael's absences and finds them to be a detriment to his progress. She is basing this on the normative Western standards of developmentally appropriate practice, because at a certain age children should be in school daily. She judges the parents for keeping him out of school for no reason. She says she knows he is lying to her when he says he is sick, because she later finds out from a sibling that the whole family went on an outing to the bowling alley. Michael knows enough to realize that Ms. Watson will not understand the cultural differences of his family structure, so he lies to her. Ms. Watson is placing her beliefs and value systems based on her knowledge of Western developmentally appropriate practices onto Michael and unfairly categorizing these differences as non-school ready.

No Time for Play

Inappropriate practices due to higher expectations and the pushing down of the curriculum directly result in less play in the early childhood classroom. Free and structured play (including: blocks, dramatic play, Legos and puppets) is no longer a part of the kindergarten and first grade day. The teacher participants have very opinionated thoughts on this new development. Participant #10 states, "I think in kindergarten you should be learning through play. You should have a kitchen area and a block area. It should not be a place where five-year-olds are sitting around holding a pencil." Thus, the new curriculum (Common Core) is inappropriate precisely because there is no more time for play. The new standards emphasize a shift to more individual instruction, a key characteristic of the neoliberal agenda. And as such there is less space for shared learning time.

In the past, according to the participating teachers, there was a Vygotskian or shared approach to learning, which gave the children more opportunities to work together and learn from one another. With this approach, learning through creative play is socially constructed and the children scaffold their knowledge through cooperative work. The teacher's role is to support the child's learning within their own ZPD (Zone of Proximal Development) so the child can co-construct meanings with others through engaging in materials (Jordan, 2009). Considerable flexibility of time in the daily schedule is needed for this approach, as its success depends on each child's particular interests and having enough time to explore different learning centers without teacher interference. Jordan states, "Co-construction thus places the emphasis on teachers and children together studying meanings in favor of acquiring facts" (Jordan, 2009, p. 43). Therefore, time is needed to co-construct meaning making through creative play and social interaction.

Ms. Watson, Ms. Moore and Ms. Springstein have all given away their blocks, Legos and all dramatic play materials. There is no time for free play or child-centered choice in kindergarten. Instead, Michael, Jay and Derek must attend to paper and pencil activities.

Michael is a creative builder. There are no longer any blocks in his room, so he builds and creatively plays with math manipulatives. He adores math time, precisely because it is one of the rare times of the day that he is allowed to physically move and create objects with materials he is allowed to explore.

Today, Ms. Watson is teaching an addition activity utilizing small plastic bees and cups. Each partnership gets to hide bees under a cup, leaving bees in front for their partner to see. If they know the total is ten, they have to count the bees in front of them and then figure out how many are hidden in the cup. Michael is hiding the bees first. His partner counts the bees that he can see and then shouts, "Five!"

"Close," says Michael, "one back from five," he hints.

"Four!" shouts his partner.

"How do you know?" asks Michael. They are both smiling wide. Michael lines the bees up and pretends they are flying in the sky.

"Buzz, buzz," he says. The other boy laughs. His partner now hides the bees under the cup and it is Michael's turn to guess.

"Five," shouts Michael, as he stacks the paper cups.

The boy nods yes.

"I saw five right here and I know five plus five is ten," he explains to his partner. Now they are both stacking the paper cups and flying the bees around the cups.

"Bum, Bada, Bum, Bum," shouts the teacher. She is eying the boys and giving them a look of disapproval. They knock down their pyramid of cups.

"Bum, bum," the class shouts. Play-time is over.

In Ms. Springstein's portable, Jay plays with paper. It is writer's workshop, and one of the only free times to explore materials openly. He cuts construction paper, glues paper on top of paper and laughs loudly. He is supposed to be writing a story, but the teacher lets the students use any writing materials they want during this time, so Jay takes advantage of it. Others are just using markers or crayons and drawing or writing on paper, but Jay is using all of the materials he can find. He likes the feel of the paper in his small hands and he rubs it up and down as he folds and cuts. This is a very tactile activity, and besides art time, this is the only time he can touch and explore materials with his fingers.

Today, Jay's teacher is having them make a mother's day gift, a cut-out colored teapot and a poem.

"Look how I am cutting out the top. . . . Now I have a poem and a teapot. . . . Everyone do this now," says Ms. Springstein. Jay is cutting intently. He is very focused. He is cutting nicely around the teapot.

"Just take your time," she says to the class.

She walks over to his table and says, "Nice job, Jay."

He smiles and takes his scrap paper and folds it neatly and stuffs it into a container in the middle of the table.

"Notice how I cut around the handle . . . watch how I cut . . . be careful as you cut . . . your job is to focus . . . don't talk to a friend. . . . It's a hard job but be careful . . ." she says to the class.

Jay pauses and puts his finger in his mouth.

"It's tricky . . . but I think you are up for the challenge," she says, still cutting her teapot in front of the classroom.

Jay's braids are shaking as he cuts. He is wearing a green shirt, jeans and cool basketball hi-tops. He bounces as he cuts. He is being very careful.

"I made a mistake," says a nearby girl.

Jay is done. He does not seem to be working too slowly.

He folds and re-folds the scraps of paper, rubbing the paper between his fingers. He picks up a pencil and writes his name on the back. He has time to explore more paper and supplies. Others have not finished cutting. He plays with the scraps and other colored paper on his table. Ms. Springstein walks by and he holds up his teapot.

"I put my name on the back," he says proudly.

"Put it on both pieces," she says.

To the whole class she says, "And then you are going to put them on my desk . . . some of you are still working and that's fine."

"I did both," he says to the boy next to him, who is not listening but talking to someone else. He walks over to the teacher.

"Where did I tell you to put that," she says loudly.

"On your desk," he replies.

"Then do it, please." Ms. Springstein seems annoyed. He puts his cut-out teapot and poem on her desk and wanders back to his table to fondle more paper.

Here, Jay is clearly proud of himself for finishing on time and wants to share his work with his teacher. She is more interested in Jay being able to follow specific directions and is annoyed when he does not.

Derek, like Michael, finds time to play during math centers. He loves touching and exploring the manipulatives. He builds with the unifix cubes, instead of counting with them, and makes patterns. He also loves to play with the geo-board, but usually gets in trouble for shooting rubber bands across the table. Quiet work time in his room is his favorite time. He gets to move from table to table and explore different materials. The only table he doesn't care for is the drawing table. He would rather move and manipulate objects.

Furthermore, the principles of free play (or creative play), which have been a part of the early childhood curriculum for generations, are now being undermined by these new regulations/standards. Many books and research studies (Chappell, 2010; Macintyre, 2016; Parks, 2014; Rogers, 2010) reveal the central importance of play in the early childhood classroom. Play, a Western construct, aids in the learning process and therefore is deemed crucial to a young child's development. It is important to note, however, that creative and free play needs to match the local cultural needs of a school's population in order for it to be pedagogically relevant.

Teacher Accountability

Over the past few years the teacher evaluation system has changed considerably in this particular school district. They have adopted the Charlotte Danielson teacher evaluation system, which is now being adopted in other big school districts nation-wide. The system scores teachers in different domains of teaching (Danielson, 2007). For example, domain 3C relates to the engagement of the students and how they respond to a lesson. It also specifically refers to transitions and how long or short transitions are in order to maximize instructional engagement. If the teacher utilizes the clock effectively, with little down time (which means more control tools), they are scored as effective (3). If, however, transitions within lessons are too long, according to the evaluator, or some children are finished before others or not engaged with the materials, the teacher is categorized as basic (2). In order for a teacher to receive a distinguished score (4), she must prove that the students themselves are monitoring their own time efficiently and are able to move on independently. Proof of this can include student checklists, preferably designed by the students themselves. This is very hard to accomplish in an early childhood classroom, as children are just learning to read and write and effectively manage their own time, and therefore have trouble actually creating their own checklists.

How does this affect an identified non-school ready child? The increased pressure of this type of accountability system directly affects how a teacher interacts with their children. For example, they may rush a child to finish a project so that they can transition more quickly to the next lesson. They can become more frustrated with a child who never finishes their work on time. And more importantly, they can see these identified non-school ready children as impeding their own evaluations as teachers.

Jay's teacher, Ms. Springstein, complains:

> So now it's going to affect my SGOs . . . someone's going to look at my class and say . . . (her name) has 11 kids below grade level not knowing that 5 of them are ADHD and only 1 is on meds . . . why do I have this low group that is not split evenly among the four of us (referring to other K teachers in Grayson).

One of the ADHD children she is referring to is Jay. He has not been diagnosed with this and perhaps the others have not either. She is just frustrated that her identified non-school ready children are going to directly affect her overall teaching score. It must be noted here that all the Grayson kindergarten teachers complain of high levels of non-school ready children, partially because they have larger class sizes than in the past (average of twenty-two with no other teacher in the room).

The end of the year score is new and more prevalent in the profession of teaching. Early childhood educators in America are now reduced to a number. Young children are also reduced to a number, and this number directly affects the evaluation score of the teacher. In lower grades, that are not considered testing grades, the number reflects the SGOs or Smart Goals, the observation scores (three per year) and the end of the year summative conference. A teacher with lower level (or identified non-school ready) children will have a lower end of the year score. A teacher with an overall score of 1 or 2 will be put on probation, even with tenure, and if they receive 1s or 2s the following year, their tenure can be challenged. Lina's teacher, Ms. Franklin, in the focus group makes it clear to the others that, "You better care about your number." This number directly relates to how a teacher is perceived by the district and is therefore actionable even if it is based on the classroom composition of students.

This means that teachers are wary of having an abundance of low-level learners or identified non-school ready children. Ms. Springstein complains that she has seven children being taken out for remediation at all points of the day. She is sure that these children will affect her score. Ms. Moore counts the number of children in remediation by looking at her coat hooks in the classroom. The last five (including Derek) are the children she has identified as non-school ready, and they all came to school after the start date. Late registration is a factor that resurfaces over and over again in this study. Children who come in after the school start date, especially in kindergarten and first grade, tend to have lower level skills. This is due to a lot of factors, which will be discussed in the next chapter, but primarily it is due to a difference in cultural expectations between the White middle class school and the variety of local cultures that have immigrated to the community.

In conclusion, higher demands and expectations driven by the implementation of the Common Core standards negatively affect young low-income Black children. As the curriculum is being pushed down and grade expectations increase (such as higher DRA scores), more young Black children will fail. Increased assessments and more indicators to grade on the report card also negatively impact the identified non-school ready child. Now, there are even more ways to fail in kindergarten. The pedagogical practices based on developmentally appropriate practices are also a huge problem, as they are geared toward Western psychology constructs and do not take into account local cultures. Increased teacher accountability measures lead to more academic pressure being placed on young children and hold the teacher specifically accountable for children that they feel will never measure up.

All of these factors directly impact the widening of the educational gap between White middle class children and low-income Black children. Black children are being identified more frequently than before, because they are not meeting these newly imposed higher standards. Therefore, these neoliberal tools are oppressive and exploitive to large groups of non-White cultures. Jay, Michael, Lina, Billy and Derek will always have trouble meeting these new expectations and as such will remain outside of mainstream schooling.

Notes

1 Guided reading consists of reading groups created by the teacher, usually by reading level.
2 SGOs are school growth outcomes, and each teacher has to have specific goals for their low, medium and high learners to attain by the end of the year.
3 ST MATH is a computer math program developed to teach basic math skills, including: addition, subtraction, number sense, shapes and etc.
4 3 is grade level, 2 is slightly below and 1 is below grade level.
5 National Association of Education for Young Children—the premier organization that accredits early care facilities.

5 Blaming the Parents

A plethora of literature squarely puts the blame for the struggling young student on the parent (Fantuzzo et al., 2004; Konald & Pianta, 2005; Ramey & Ramey, 2004; Wright, 2001; Wu & Qi, 2006). Within this study, I uncover this deficit-based theory to be prevalent. Teacher participants are following this normative discourse. This is a complex narrative, because at points they say they understand their parents' lack of involvement (due to long work schedules), but at the same time, they are unknowingly perpetuating this deficit parent discourse by demanding that they conform to the values of school culture.

In this chapter, I examine the issue of parental blame and how it impacts the lives of low-income Black families and in particular these five children. The factors included in this analysis are: the issue of parental involvement or non-involvement, low wage jobs and inflexible schedules, extended kinship networks, the value of education, late registration, unequal childhoods and the question of cultural capital and differing expectations between the teacher and the family.

Parental Involvement

The expectation of all of the participating teachers is that ALL parents will be involved in their child's schooling experience. This is a non-negotiable expectation and is related to the dominant cultural values of the school system. A lot of research supports this adamant stance (Epstein et al., 2009; Robinson & Harris, 2014 and more), and they all advocate a strong home–school connection. This directly refers to the expectation of high parental involvement.

The survey I conduct in this district reveals that these teachers wholeheartedly agree with this literature and believe that parents should be actively involved in the classroom and their child's school progress. Of the teachers that respond to this survey, 81.82% indicate that it is very important for parents of the identified non-school ready child to be actively involved in their classroom. Another 88.36% say that parents should attend all Back to School nights and parent teacher conferences in order to stay on top of their child's progress. In contrast, only 4.5% of these same teachers say that the parents of their non-school ready children are actively involved in their schooling. This illustrates that although the kindergarten and first grade teachers feel it is very important for parents to participate, the identified non-school ready child's parents are not participating at all, or only rarely.

Jay's parents have not come in to school all year. Jay's grandmother picks him up from school on a daily basis. Ms. Springstein sends home notes and even calls home, but rarely gets a chance to talk to the parents. After the second parent teacher conference, to which they do not show up at the assigned time, she calls them and leaves an urgent message. She needs to talk to them about Jay's lack of progress. She is afraid she may have to retain him. She asks them to come in for a brief sit down. The father shows up a week later. He has left work in the middle of one of his three shifts as a driver for a major cola company. He can get into trouble, but he realizes that the teacher really needs to speak to him. They meet and she tells him her concerns. He understands and tells her he trusts her ability to make the best decision for Jay. He is a high school drop-out himself and never did well in school, so he is not surprised Jay is having issues. Later, Ms. Springstein reveals to me that this brief meeting upsets her with his parents. She is frustrated. She can't get them to do extra work with him at home and Jay never does his homework.

Ironically, even though she is frustrated and being somewhat judgmental of the parents' involvement, she understands the overall situation. When I ask her if she thinks socio-economic class is a factor in whether a child comes to school ready or not, she responds immediately, saying:

> I think it's a factor because I think both parents are working. Parents are working three and four jobs to live in this town so their kids can go to this school. It's expensive to live in this town . . . even over in our neighborhood (all Black lower-income section) the rent is really high. So it's not that they don't want to help their kids . . . they are probably not even home at night . . . they are exhausted.

In other words, Ms. Springstein has some understanding that there are valid reasons why these parents are not available to help their children after school or participate in daily class activities. This comment illustrates that she is aware of the investment and sacrifices low-income parents make in order to provide quality education for their young children. Just two blocks away is an urban school district that is known for low-quality educational practices, and these parents (including Jay's) do not want to send their children to these schools. The close proximity of this urban school district might be a factor as to why the parents choose to spend a little more on rent to be in this particular township.

Lina's teacher, Ms. Franklin agrees. She says:

> Well I would say it (socio-economic class) plays a huge part in school readiness, because there's no one reading to the child at home. . . .

They are working all the time. They are not home. They (the identified non-school ready child) are being picked up by neighbors . . . daycare and there is nobody really holding them accountable for things either.

Ms. Franklin, again, has some understanding of why these parents are not always around. She knows they are working many different low-wage jobs in order to make ends meet. Yet, she still has an expectation of parental involvement based on her own middle class value system (Dodson, 2009)

Even though there is some understanding of how these parents (who are low-income) need to work many hours in order to survive, they all still expect full parental involvement. "I have a parent I have only met once this year," states Ms. Springstein, and I am not sure if she is referring to Jay or another child. Ms. Moore, Derek's teacher, also laments seeing very few parents of the identified non-school ready children in her classroom. With the increase of demands from the district, they are even more disappointed with the lack of parental involvement. They need the parents' help in order to reach their own SGOs and provide evidence of progress in reading and math. They believe that if a six-year-old practices reading every night with his parent, it will help increase the child's DRA levels, and rightfully so. They feel so overwhelmed with having to do it all themselves.

Dodson's research reveals that there is a direct correlation between higher standards and demands on teachers and the teachers' increase in blaming the parent for not being involved (Dodson, 2009). However, Dodson and others (Hale, 2001) believe that this disparity of parental involvement in lower income non-White households is widely misunderstood and unsupported. The realities are that time is highly constrained for parents of low-income non-White families, and therefore they should not be judged negatively for non-participation. Also, non-participation does not mean that these parents do not care about their child's educational progress. It may just mean they can't get out of work in order to physically be there in the school in order to meet with the teacher.

Low-Wage Jobs and Inflexible Schedules

Parents of identified non-school ready children are largely low-income and therefore must work multiple jobs or shifts because their jobs are low-wage and do not pay livable wages. They need as many hours as possible in order to make enough money to support their families. They are mostly in the service, retail or caregiving industries and receive minimum wage ($7–8 per hour) with no benefits (Ehrenreich & Hochschild, 2004; Luttrell & Dodson, 2011; Polakow, 2007).

Jay's dad works for a large soda company driving their delivery trucks. He puts in long hours and multiple shifts per day to help pay the bills. He is an hourly employee, and only gets paid when he is at work. His wife works on the retail side of the same soda company and is attending school at night, aiming for an associates degree in healthcare. She does not get any sick days or vacation days and again only gets paid for the hours she works.

Derek's mom, who speaks little to no English, is in the caregiving sector, working long hours as a home aid for an elderly woman. She is the sole provider and must work another job later in the afternoon at a senior center. She can't take any time off of work, even for Derek's kindergarten promotion ceremony, because every penny counts. She has relatives nearby that help her with Derek and a community of Haitian immigrant neighbors who also help out when necessary. In many cases like hers, the mother is the sole provider (85% of low-income Black families are headed by a single mother) (Harry & Klingner, 2006). They need to work even longer hours in order to provide for their families. Dodson notes that there is a disproportionately higher population of women of color and immigrants working in these low-wage sectors (Dodson, 2009).

Low-wage work is highly time consuming, because it takes several different jobs or multiple shifts in order to make enough money to pay the bills. In Ehrenreich's research, she herself takes an eye-opening journey into the world of low-wage work and proves categorically that it is very hard for one person, let alone two people, who are receiving minimum wage forty hours per week to make enough money to survive (Ehrenreich, 2011). If two parents (i.e., Jay's parents) are both earning $8 per hour for forty hours per week, their combined annual income would be $34,000, which is below the poverty line for a family of four (Dodson, 2009). It is important to note here that Jay has two younger siblings, so there are five people in his family at this time, not including extended family members.

Another problem with low-wage work is transportation to and from work. Only one family out of the five studied has a car (Lina). This is interesting because Lina's parents are the most involved in their child's schooling. They come in regularly to meetings and are able to show up at night, largely because they can get to and from work more easily. The others all rely on public transportation to get to and from work. This is costly and also takes up a lot of time. This is actually one of the reasons Derek's mom cites that she can't make it back in time to pick up Derek from the school bus. She has to take two buses to her morning job and two buses to return. Later on, she has to get back on the bus to go to her afternoon/night job.

Furthermore, low-wage jobs do not offer any flexibility in scheduling. Most low-wage jobs actually have inconsistent scheduling that does not provide workers with set hours week to week. Inflexibility in scheduling means that it is hard to schedule appointments with teachers in advance. It is also hard for a worker to know ahead of time if they can take time off to visit a school production or performance. Billy's mom has moved a lot and is new to the area. She can't afford to lose her new job working in retail. She does not have a set schedule and therefore each week does not know when she will be going to work. Sometimes she closes the store and has to stay late and sometimes she needs to arrive early to open the store. She works six days a week, and takes as many shifts as she can get. She has trouble scheduling anything with Ms. Smith because she only knows her schedule less than a week in advance. Ms. Smith tries to accommodate her by getting to work earlier, but Billy's mom has been a no-show twice already.

Since there is no job security, these parents can't afford to be sick. They usually go in anyway because they have to. Sometimes, Michael's mom calls out just to be with the family. They spend quality family time together, and Michael and his brother miss school. She understands the importance of spending time with family and she misses her boys a lot. So they go bowling instead of her going to work. She calls in sick and she tells the boys to tell their teachers that they are sick too. She is taking a risk. She can get fired at any time from her caregiver job.

Jay can be sick in the middle of the day and has to wait for hours in the nurse's office because no one can pick him up. If his grandma is at work too, he needs to wait until she comes home. Many children of low-wage earners spend hours waiting to be picked up. The school calls everyone on the emergency contact form but may still not reach anybody. And even if they do, the parent will say that they can't pick them up right away because they are at work. Sometimes a neighbor has to come by and pick up the child because the parents can't come at all. They will lose pay if they leave work, and there is no guarantee that they will not be fired for walking out of the job.

Extended Kinship Networks

Low-wage work and working multiple shifts/jobs demand extended kinship networks. Parents in these circumstances are not always around, so they rely on others for childcare and support. Someone has to pick up the kids from school or aftercare, and sometimes a family member or a neighbor fills that role. Extended kin are also often needed to take the child to school and before-care, as work shifts can also be early in the morning. Derek and Billy arrive early for before-care and have breakfast each day before school. Jay tries to make it to breakfast too, but is late a lot depending on how tired his mom is from going to her own school the night before.

The teachers in this study complain that their low-income Black families, who hail from a variety of cultures, are not able to personally pick up their children from school on a regular basis. They cite this as an issue, because they do not have regular interaction with the parent. When speaking about Derek, Ms. Moore points out:

> Someone else is picking up the kid . . . this person picks him up on Mondays . . . this person picks him up on Tuesdays and then a cousin comes and when they get home the mom is at work.

This working parent strategy (in this case, low-income Black parents) does not line up with the expectations of White middle class teachers. These teachers prefer a partnership with the parent, and if a parent is not consistently picking up the child, it is harder for them to communicate regularly.

Ms. Moore and the other teachers are also frustrated that these children stay at other people's houses, which makes it harder for them to consistently finish their homework. "I see them staying at grandmas . . . or their aunts," says Ms. Moore, who feels that this interferes with their academic progress. The teachers' expectation that one of the parents pick up the child every day stems from their own backgrounds. Each of the teachers in this study had a mom who stayed home, picked them up at school and was actively engaged in their schooling. Therefore, they base this expectation on their own family structure, which stems from White middle class norms (Cannella, 1997; Hale, 2001; Randolph, 2013).

However, family dynamics and household structures may look different in low-income Black households where parents hold multiple low-wage jobs. They are more likely to include extended family members, which can lead to more interaction with different relatives. Children who live in large households learn how to mediate and are very group orientated, which is a positive life skill (Hale, 2001; Hale-Benson & Hilliard, 1986). Such group interaction and the import placed on being part of a group are contrary to the Western notions of childhood and the importance of the individual. As a result, the ability to navigate a larger group is downplayed in Western culture and is perceived as different and unworthy. Stack (1975) found that kinship networks exist within low-income Black neighborhoods and the 'swapping' of goods and services is an obligatory practice. Childcare is not restricted to a nuclear family structure, but is extended to all kin, including trusted friends and neighbors (Stack, 1975). There is a notably different rhythm to everyday life because of this extended kinship network (Lareau & Weininger, 2008). An uncle or a neighbor may pick up a Black young child from school one day, and the great-grandmother the next, as they are all working together to raise the child.

Extended kinship networks are therefore essential to the survival of low-wage work families, as they can't simply take a day off of work if a child is sick. They have no sick days or job security. They need others to help out in many instances, including: drop off, pick-up, when a child gets sick at school, opening school delays, vacation days, early dismissal and snow days.

The Stigma of Low-Wage Work

Low-wage jobs in the retail, service and caregiving sectors are not deemed to be 'good' jobs by other professionals. Workers in these fields are paid less than professional sectors and therefore are stigmatized as being less worthy to the overall economy structure. Occupational status is important, and does affect how a professional teacher/educator responds to a family and their child. If you are a professional, such as a doctor, lawyer, teacher, accountant, you garner community support and respect, but if you work at the local McDonald's or nearby soda manufacturer, you might be considered unworthy or lacking in job status. Parents in such jobs (Jay's, Derek's, Billy's and Michael's) must deal with the everyday stigma attached to low-wage work. Lina's mom is in the secretarial profession, which is also highly underpaid but has less stigma attached.

In any case, all of these parents are not considered professionals by any standards. Teachers like to think that they do not judge the professions of their families, but they do. Again, they are utilizing a White middle class lens when responding to professions outside of their own realms and as such, knowingly or not, tend to make negative judgments. Their parents did not work for a soda company driving a truck. Interestingly, all five teachers in the interview study make it clear that their moms stayed home and did not work. Their fathers were the bread-winners (very heteronormative) and worked in professional jobs. Thus, they do not have any real exposure to low-wage work, which means that they do not completely understand what it entails in everyday life.

The Value of Education

The teachers in this study unknowingly contribute to this discourse of attaching blame to low-wage parents because they feel that there is less interest in the child's education. When discussing Derek's mom and other children from low-wage immigrant homes, Ms. Moore states, "School is not . . . it appears to me that school is not as important as it should be." Ms. Springstein and Ms. Watson both agree with this sentiment. Ms. Springstein states: "And some of the parents are like . . . well they can miss school. It's just kindergarten, so they can miss it. Well you are missing a lot of kindergarten." Absences are an important issue with these teachers, and they feel that it relates to how much or how little the parent/family values education. Again there is an intrinsic conflict in these teachers' responses. They say they understand the necessary amount of work the parents and family members need to do in order to survive, but they also crave a family–school partnership that centers on valuing their children's education.

Ms. Smith doesn't think that Billy's mom values his education at all. She knows that the mom is busy working, but she has trouble personally relating to the mom not showing up to valuable school meetings. She, herself, has two children, both in elementary school, and she has never missed a scheduled teacher meeting.

Ms. Watson thinks that Michael's record of increased absences reveals his mother's lack of commitment to his academic progress. She believes that if the mom really did value his education, then she would work on improving his reading and writing skills every night. She has three daughters herself, and works with them each night on academic projects. It is hard for her to relate to Michael's mom's lack of involvement or interest in her child's education.

In contrast, Ms. Franklin believes that Lina's parents do care and value her educational progress, and yet she does not agree with what they qualify as educational progress. She feels that Lina lacks the background knowledge that is needed to attend first grade, and therefore she is behind in all subjects. Interestingly, Lina's parents do not agree with this assessment and instead are very happy with her progress in her old daycare classroom. This difference in expectation of a child's educational progress can be interpreted as the parents not valuing education in general.

Late Registration

The teachers all connect the issue of late registration to the parent's lack of valuing education. Again, they are all utilizing a lens of White middle class values, which inevitably leads to the perpetuation of parental blame.

When a child starts school later, perhaps even just a few days late, it is harder for the teacher to complete all of the proper assessments on that child. Furthermore, if the child comes to school later, they did not come to the kindergarten orientation a few months before, and have not been assessed with *school readiness* assessments, such as the Brigance. This means the teachers have not been able to score the child based on this screening, and therefore evenly distribute the lower level children throughout the various kindergarten classes.

All of the teachers in this study blame the low-wage parent for not registering their children on time. Registration starts in February of the previous school year and runs through the end of August, giving parents seven months to register in time for school. Ms. Watson states:

> The parents need to know that I am moving into a community. It's their responsibility. We can't just keep saying they don't know . . . they don't know.

Ms. Watson believes that immigrant parents coming in from another country (Africa, Haiti, Jamaica, etc.) must somehow quickly adapt to the new laws and regulations of their new homeland. When I point out that they may not know English (like Derek's mom), she shrugs and makes it clear that that is their job to learn English and to find out the practices and customs of their new town.

Ms. Moore, Derek's teacher and others make a direct correlation to late registration and non-school readiness. Her coat rack tells her how many children are identified as non-school ready in her classroom because they all registered late. Derek is one of her last hooks on the coat rack. When I ask her about the connection between these two issues, she states:

> I feel that parents that don't register their children for school aren't doing their best to get them ready for school.

It is that simple. They don't care, so they don't register in time. This then brings the blame fully on the parent.

Unequal Childhoods

Parents who work low-wage jobs have less access to the educational process. In addition to time constraints posed by working multiple jobs/shifts, they lack the cultural capital to fully navigate their children's schooling. According to Lareau (2003), in her research on families from differing socio-economic classes, low-wage earners live by a different childrearing logic and this affects their interaction with schools. Lareau defines these differences with the term 'concerted cultivation,' which is the art of being able to engage in cultural capital. Middle and upper socio-economic families are able to fully utilize these skills in their interaction with the school/educational system. They teach their children the art of negotiation and give them a sense of entitlement that helps both the child and the parent navigate the world of school (Lareau, 2003). Therefore, these parents actively engage in schoolwork in and outside of the school itself. Teachers, who are also primarily White and middle class, understand and expect these same values from all children, regardless of their socio-economic background.

When speaking about Derek, Ms. Moore states:

> There's not a lot of talking about school or even doing homework together or any books being read to them before bedtime . . . or a bedtime routine which I think is very important to be ready for school. Get ready and get into bed . . . let's have a story. Tell me what you did today . . .

Ms. Moore is unknowingly projecting her own middle class logic of concerted cultivation as the cornerstone of childrearing practices onto the expectations of her parents. Her expectations are based on middle class values, and she believes all families, regardless of socio-economic backgrounds, should be incorporating the same values at home. She does not know what specific rituals Derek and his mom attend to before bed, but she is sure that it lacks educational value.

According to Lareau, low-income families follow a different childrearing logic. They are committed to providing basic services, such as food and shelter for their children (Lareau, 2003). They do not have the money or the time to take children to dance classes or museum outings, but instead give them space to grow and learn by themselves, which she refers to as an accomplishment of natural growth (Lareau, 2003).

Providing a sense of entitlement and verbal negotiation skills gives the middle class child an advantage inside the institution of school. Low-income children, on the other hand, speak up less and rarely challenge or question the authority figures in their world. This may contribute to why the five children in this study participate less in the classroom. There is a general acceptance of directives and they generally do not negotiate or reason with their parents or authority figures. All of the children in this study are well behaved at home and respect their elders. However, they have more free time to interact within extended kinship networks in order to promote their own natural growth.

Ultimately, however, there is a distinct advantage for the middle class child within the institution of school. The cultivation of time-consuming leisure activities works to their advantage, as does their ability to verbally negotiate. They are able to talk at length about a subject and are able to communicate with more confidence. When discussing her students' verbal abilities, Ms. Moore states,

> I think what happens at home determines if you are ready for school. If you are having discussions with your parents . . . it doesn't have to be a discussion but if your parents are talking to you . . . if they are saying it's summertime . . . it's hot in the summer . . . just one sentence. I feel like a lot of homes are missing that talk.

Ms. Moore's understanding of what happens at home is laced with concerted cultivation logic, as she feels that there should be more discussions between parent and child at home. Clearly, she feels that Derek needs an English-speaking mother to verbally interact with him at home on a regular basis.

In general, low-income children display many more constraints in their interaction in school settings (Lareau, 2003). They enjoy less success making the rules in their favor because they have not been trained to question authority. They also may not feel as valued or heard (like their parents) because of this difference in childrearing logic. They have trouble advocating for themselves and do not always have the communication skills necessary to explain their problems or issues with school. This may be why Ms. Franklin gets so frustrated with Lina. She wants her to openly value and utilize more words to convey her thoughts and feelings, but Lina has trouble speaking her mind. This can lead to frustration and alienation within the cultural systems of the school. This is the case with Lina's parents, who believe there may be a racial issue involved with their daughter being pulled out for Academic Intervention. They are unhappy with the placement and are frustrated that the teacher does not ask for their input.

Low-wage parents also exhibit less skill and knowledge in advocating for their children in school. Knowing and understanding the culture of the school is essential to navigating it and advocating for your child. This includes being aware of social expectations and having time to attend parent teacher meetings. This inability to properly advocate for their children is one reason for the high referral rates of low-income Black students to special education settings. Low-income parents do not always know their rights and therefore may not contest or question special education referrals. Derek's mom, who comes to one intervention with a relative (to be her translator), is unsure of her rights as his parent and does not understand why they are even meeting. Harry and Klingner (2006) refer to this as a culture of referral, as their research reveals high referral rates (up to 50% per class) of students in all-Black schools to the special education team. Parents who are low-wage earners do not always show up to these referral/ determination meetings, and as a result forfeit their right to be a part of the process (Harry & Klingner, 2006).

An example of this is a parent of one of my first graders. She has been incommunicado for a couple of months because she's working three seasonal jobs a day. Thus, she is not able to make the intervention meeting scheduled with me, the vice-principal and members of the special education team. She actually calls the school twenty minutes before the meeting to say she's unable to leave work to make the meeting. In this case, the vice principal and the head social worker discuss educational negligence in her absence. The reading interventionist reports that she can never reach the mom and it's clear that the child is not reading at home with the grandma. I am asked if I observe help or support at home and I (although conflicted) say no. The child's residence in town is then questioned, since the mother's no longer picking her up from school. The social worker immediately contacts the district office to have her address checked. This all happens within ten minutes of the mother not showing up for this important meeting. This example illustrates how quickly a working mother can be wrongfully judged as uninterested or uncommitted to her child's educational progress. (This child was then removed from my class a month later, citing residence issues.) This scenario could fit Jay, Billy, Derek or Michael too. And it may play out later in their schooling years.

Differing Expectations

Even though the teacher participants have some understanding that parents can not physically be at home because they are working long hours, they still believe that the parents should be more involved in the social and academic progress of their non-school ready children. By expressing these views, they are unknowingly holding all parents to the same standard of behavior, regardless of socio-economic class or cultural background. This means that low-income families from differing cultures will always fall short and be blamed for not following middle class mores.

In their background interviews, all of the participating teachers stress the importance of their own parents' involvement in their educational lives. Their parents attended all school functions, came to parent teacher conferences and were seen in and around the school building on a regular basis.

When I ask Ms. Franklin if she has a theory about why certain children are starting school non-school ready, she replies:

> My theory is that parents who read to their children all the time and that are home talking to their children . . . and parents that are taking them to parks, museums and places and you know . . . are having a lot of learning experiences at a very early age . . . I think generally do . . . are more ready for school.

It is interesting to note that Ms. Franklin starts to say 'they generally do' and then switches to 'are more ready for school,' which sounds like a more equitable and non-predictive comment to make about a child. Through her comments, she reveals an awareness of a possible deficit relationship to a differing childrearing logic.

The following excerpt from an interview with Ms. Franklin reveals this difference in childrearing practices/expectations:

Me: So you think it's on the parents?

Ms. Franklin: I think it's partially . . . mostly . . . I think it's very helpful for parents to do that (referring to above statement) . . . that generally speaking. . . . Parents . . . I don't care . . . you know how much money they make or whatever . . . if you give your children . . . the time and the reading and the experiences than I think children generally are more school ready . . .

Me: Well, you are talking about middle class values though . . .

Ms. Franklin: It's everyone's values, right?

Me: Middle class values are everyone's values? Interesting?

Here, Ms. Franklin is equating the middle class system of educational expectations with values that she feels are appropriate for all cultures/ backgrounds. All the participating teachers are operating under this same assumption, that middle class values are everyone's values, but this is short-sighted and not inclusive of the varying populations that attend this school.

The theme of childrearing expectations that are based on dominant Western practices relates to Gupta's research (2006) on early childhood teachers and how they insert their own values and logic of childrearing in their teacher training and classroom practices. According to her, teachers construct knowledge through their own ideological ideas based on their backgrounds (Gupta, 2006). They may be unaware that they transfer their own values and ideologies about parenting onto the families they serve. This research relates directly to the population of teachers that participated in this study, as they, too, have specific ideas/expectations shaped by their own White middle class upbringings that are placed on the differing cultures of the populations they serve.

A good example of this difference in expectation is reading. Developing a love of reading is a fundamental part of these teachers' shared value system. They grew up with parents who valued reading and modeled their love of books daily. Books surrounded them and were an integral part of their growing up years.

Jay's teacher, Ms. Springstein recalls:

> I grew up to appreciate reading . . . I remember as a child . . . where I would . . . we had a huge house. It was a really big house. I can remember walking through our living room and going to our television room and my mother was reading . . . so reading was very important.

She observed that reading was important to her mother and therefore she accepted it as a great importance in her life. Ms. Franklin also recalls the importance of reading in her home as a child and in her home presently while raising her own two children.

> My mother was a big reader . . . I just remember her always reading . . . reading all the time. She was always curled up with a book and she was reading to us. And now everyone's a big reader in my family . . . I made sure I read a lot in front of them . . . so they can always say 'my mother is always reading'. . . . Maybe I subconsciously did it . . . I don't know. . . . It's just that books are very important.

Clearly, Ms. Franklin feels obliged to share certain values from her own childhood with her children, including her love of reading/books. These values affect how she observes and interacts in the world around her. Like the other participating teachers, nurturing an interest in books and reading remains an important part of Ms. Franklin's present value system.

This White middle class expectation of parents reading to their child on a nightly basis clashes with the everyday practical nature of most low-income families. There simply is no time for reading. Books are also expensive, and thus there are not a lot available inside these children's homes. Libraries are the only possible way to procure books; yet dwindling public library hours and overdue fines are a deterrent to families that cannot get there too frequently.

Jay, Michael, Billy and Derek only see books in school. They do not have books in their house, and in Derek's case there are no English reading materials either. Their parents are working too hard and long to read to them or work with them on their homework. They do not see their mothers sitting around curled up reading a book. Their parents did not grow up with books on their shelves either. There are different cultural expectations. And in this case their parents believe that reading and love of books is the job of the school and not the home. They do not have the same expectations of reading and schoolwork at home. And this is a problem for White middle class early childhood educators.

This is not to say that there is no early literacy learning in low-income non-White homes, but this is how it appears to the White middle class teacher who has no knowledge of the cultural value systems of other non-dominant cultures. Mercado (2005) critically analyzes the deficit assumption that children who do not have books in their house are not actively involved in acquiring literacy skills. Instead, she documents a case study within Puerto Rican homes in New York City that actually reveal literacy knowledge, just in different forms. Children in her study learn about reading and other literacy skills through oral language/story-telling, reading and critically analyzing the bible, reading Spanish news-papers, practicing phonics skills and continual translation of words from Spanish to English in writing (Mercado, 2005). This is just one example of a Funds of Knowledge[1] discourse within a culture that is overlooked and not valued as important within the dominant White middle class discourse on literacy.

The participating teachers complain about the Nigerian and Haitian parents because these parents expect all schoolwork to be done in school. In other words, they do not understand when the teacher asks them to do more reading or work at home because they feel that this is the sole function of the school and does not belong in the home. White middle class teachers in general are seeking mutual partnerships with parents and therefore are disappointed when a parent points out that reading and the practice of reading is the teacher's job, in a school environment.

Ms. Moore states:

> In the beginning of school she (Derek's mom) said 'you make him behave' . . . she said to me . . . and I say 'it's kinda of like a village' and 'you're the teacher' (she says) 'you teach him and then I come and pick him up and take him home . . .'

Good behavior, in this case and with other Haitian parents, is the focus. The expectation is that the American school will help the child to achieve success. They have high expectations of good behavior and sometimes only want to hear about that, and not about their academic progress. The teachers become frustrated when they encounter different cultures that believe that education is the responsibility of the school and not the family.

According to Hale's research (2001), this is primarily a clash of expectations between the White middle class-based values of the school and other cultures. Hale advocates for a change in White teachers' expectations, because as it stands now, the middle class White family is able to meet these teachers' expectations, yet low-income non-White populations have less success. I agree with this assertion and believe that this leads to a widening of the gap between these different populations. Low-income non-White families who have different cultural expectations will always be considered deficient (or non-school ready) within this framework.

Lina does not do her homework. Actually she has been crumpling up the homework sheets and stuffing them behind the computer desk in the classroom for a while now. Ms. Franklin has been calling the parents for months. She doesn't understand why they are not helping her with her schoolwork at home. In an interview, she complains about the teacher having to do it all. She needs Lina's parents to cooperate, and they are not doing what she feels is needed at home. When discussing Lina and her parents, she states:

> My job is to take care of everything that happens at school and she (Lina) doesn't do her homework. . . . So I am always talking to her mom about that. She says she asked her (Lina) if she did her homework so she thinks she (Lina) is doing her homework.

Ms. Franklin is unable to understand why Lina's mom is not more on top of the homework. She would not necessarily believe her own child when they say they have done their homework. She checks the homework herself. Middle class parents sometimes sign homework sheets to let the teacher know that they are aware of their child doing homework. She is astounded that Lina's mom does not even question where the homework has been for months. Ms. Franklin finally finds the waded up homework sheets and still does not get the response from the parents she feels is appropriate.

Teachers are expecting partnerships with parents, and whether they realize it or not, when they do not get this in some form or another, they blame the parent. When discussing Michael's family, Ms. Watson states:

> And if there is a parent who is just waiting for school to teach them (the children) everything . . . that's what I find. I find that there's a lot of parents that just assume . . . wait until school and they will teach them what they need to know . . .

In this instance, the White middle class teacher has certain expectations based on her own value system that interferes with her working relationship with parents from differing backgrounds and cultures. Ms. Watson does not understand how a parent could actually do nothing in preparing their child for school. And clearly she feels that these parents are deficient in their understanding of the structure of school itself. It is important to note that this feeling only gets exacerbated with higher standards and accountability structures, as the teacher feels like they cannot do all of the work by themselves. Now more than ever, parents are expected to help out in the learning process, which can be a burden on other cultural value systems.

In summary, although the participating teachers are aware that low-income parents are working many jobs, they still expect more involvement in the educational process. Jay's, Derek's, Billy's, Michael's and Lina's parents are trapped in low-wage jobs working multiple shifts in order to pay the bills. They are in constant fear of losing their jobs if they take time off for school meetings or events. They also lack the cultural capital that is necessary to navigate the school system. Expectations can be different due to cultural differences. Parents who emigrate from other countries, such as Haiti and Nigeria, have different expectations of schooling and their own involvement in their child's schooling. Also, the teachers in this study are interested in a mutual partnership based on Western middle class values and are disappointed when these parents are not physically available to support their children academically. Unknowingly, these teachers, and others like them, are actually widening the gap educationally between White middle class children and low-income non-White children, as these parents do not fulfill their expectations. In a way it is a set-up for failure, and the identified non-school ready child (who is low-income and non-White) pays the price. Deficit constructs are again perpetuated and more developed, and now the identification of non-school readiness is based on differing standards/ practices.

Note

1 Funds of Knowledge are a pedagogical practice that involves ongoing mutual relationships with families and local communities. Families share their knowledge systems/culture with the classroom.

6 Young Black Lives Matter

Young Black lives matter is a term I have borrowed from the Black Lives Matter movement that was started in response to the 2012 non-guilty verdict in the shooting and death of Trayvon Martin. It is a national organization that works 'toward the validity of Black life.' This book is also a call to action and responds to the present crisis in the Black liberation movement of Black Lives Matter.

In this chapter I unpack and examine the complex understandings and multiple layers of race and how race directly relates to *school readiness* discourse. During this study, different discourses on race emerged, including: color-blind discourse and other race ideologies, White discomfort/White fragility, race and meritocracy and race as it relates to socio-economic status. The findings reveal the complexity of the issue of race and how it directly relates to the classification/identification process of *school readiness* in young non-White children.

I, myself, grew up in a predominantly all Black community in Brooklyn, New York during the White flight of the 1970s. I was one of two White children in my elementary school classroom, and at times it made me uncomfortable. My mom worked at an all Black college and I was always the outsider, the minority, the other. My mom felt that being Jewish helped her gain acceptance into this all-Black world, as she grew up feeling different and outside the mainstream, too. When I was younger and living in Ohio, we struggled with anti-Semitic comments and actions by our neighbors. I remember my mom telling me that I should be proud of my race (she considered Judaism a race) and that I would someday fit in with others. It should be noted here that when Jews immigrated (mostly late 1800s and 1900s), they were considered non-White (Roediger, 2005). My grandparents were immigrants from Russia and Poland and left many family members behind who were killed, precisely because of their race, by the Germans during World War II. This history is probably why my mom also talked about Judaism as a race and not just as a religion or ethnicity.

This experience helped me navigate my world in Brooklyn where I had a different skin color. I felt more accepted, interestingly enough, in the Black world of Brooklyn than I previously felt in the all-White Christian world of Ohio.

As I got older I realized that I felt uncomfortable when Black people were absent from the geographical space around me. I still feel this way when I travel and am more aware of this today, as my spouse is Black and my two children are bi-racial. Even with this unique upbringing, I still experience moments of discomfort around issues of race, because I am not Black and do not fully understand what is it like to be Black in our society. Furthermore, as a White teacher in a classroom where fifteen out of twenty-one children are Black, I reflect on this issue daily and wonder how it affects my perceptions of and assumptions about *school readiness*. Frankenberg's research reveals that "race shapes White women's lives" (Frankenberg, 1993, p. 1). It has definitely shaped my life, as well as the lives of the teacher participants in this study.

Race Ideologies

Frankenberg's research (1993) identifies three possible race ideologies that White women adhere to in discussions on race: 'essentialist racism,' 'color evasion/power evasion' and 'race cognizant' (Frankenberg, 1993). This is key to understanding how these five 'non-school ready' low-income Black children are being viewed/perceived in their classrooms.

Essentialist racism is what the United States is founded upon. It utilizes race as a hierarchal structure and emphasizes biological differences that are deficit-based. This is bound up in the historical/economic structure of slavery and how the law positioned slaves as less than a whole person. It is, however, still in practice, and is sometimes more evident within its practices. For example, Jim Crow laws and segregated schools are a part of essentialist racism, and so are the more recent political views of Republican presidential candidates (e.g., Donald Trump). It espouses White supremacy and negates other cultures, such as Muslims (who are profiled as terrorists) and Latino immigrants. At one Trump rally, he stated, "When Mexico sends its people, they're not sending the best. . . . They are sending people that have lots of problems. They are bringing drugs, they are bringing crime. They are rapists and some I assume are good people" (CNN.com, 2015). He talks about building a wall and keeping these 'criminals/rapists' out of America. These are all examples of explicit forms of racism that are more obvious and less subtle in practice.

Errold Bailey (2015) contends that colonialism and the institution of slavery have directly produced conditions within our school system that result in an achievement gap between the two races. This is another example of essentialist racist ideology because the racist conditions of the past "indicate the hegemonic practices and features of slavery and colonialism produce institutionalized and internalized consequences that continue to affect educational outcomes" (Bailey, 2015, p. 1). Here, he provides a direct connection between the overt racist structures of the past (colonialism and slavery) and how they currently affect racist structural practices and policies in schools today (Race to the Top/No Child Left Behind).

Color evasion/power evasion emphasizes sameness in all humans and renders race a non-issue. This is known as color-blindness and is more commonly utilized through White discourse than race essentialism, mainly because White people do not want to be classified as racist. It, however, is still racist, because it negates differences and pretends that there is no race-related issue within a historically racist structure. The system of racism is invisible and therefore embedded in the institution of the school (Bonilla-Silva, 2006; Frankenberg, 1993; Leonardo, 2009, 2013; Randolph, 2013).

Color-blind discourse is built into academic standards. Unbeknownst to the teachers in this study, they perpetuate color-blindness by trying to meet the higher demands of the district. There is no time to differentiate between children, as they are all expected to meet the new standards, regardless of the history of racial marginalization within the educational system. Thus, a low-income Black child (Billy) who has had no preschool experience is expected to achieve the same level in reading by the end of first grade as a White middle class child in his class who attended a top tier preschool. Furthermore, Billy's teacher, Ms. Smith, who is wrapped up in the district discourse of expectations/high standards, does not necessarily realize that Billy, because he is Black and from a low-income family, is more likely to be classified as non-school ready. She simply sees that he is not meeting the standards of the grade and is far behind the other students. Interestingly, when I ask her about race and if it affects the identification of *school readiness*, Ms. Smith sees no correlation between the two:

> I don't think so . . . because it can't be . . . but I have seen families . . . different races of families that are . . . even if they might not speak the language. . . . There is a pride in education . . . education and learning and a respect for the school community. . . . I just don't see it that way because I have taught all the colors of the rainbow kids . . .

Ms. Smith is unaware that she is on some level perpetuating a color-blind discourse with her comment that she "has taught all the colors of the rainbow kids" and feels that race is a non-issue as long as the child's parents take pride in education.

This is a common reaction of all the teacher participants in this study, as they are more focused on meeting the high expectations of the district rather than examining the social structures in a color-blind society. In a district-wide survey of K/1 teachers, 81.82% believe that the teacher should make sure their class knows that they are all the same even if they are different skin colors. This conveys sameness of all. For example, Jay and Lina are African American and have relatives that were slaves in the United States, whereas Derek is from Haiti, as are all of his relatives, some who still live there in poverty. Billy's family is from Western Africa originally and has a very different family past/structure. Thus, even the Black children in this study are from a variety of cultures and are not all the same.

Bonilla-Silva (2006) contends that at the heart of color-blind discourse lies the myth that racism is a thing of the past. Slavery is over and so is legally sanctioned segregation, so now White people can believe that race is no longer a legitimate issue within American society. He critically states, "The idea that race has all but disappeared as a factor shaping the lives of Americans" (Bonilla-Silva, 2006, p. 208). This color-blind discourse maintains and perpetuates White privilege in the early childhood classroom. This relates to Lina's parents' concerns that race may be a factor in Lina's placement in Academic Intervention. Ms. Franklin is horrified to hear this (from another parent) because she feels that her judgment/classification has nothing to do with race.

A condition of this color-blind discourse is "White Habitus." A part of this is Whites are not around Blacks on a regular basis. Bonilla-Silva found that fewer than 10% of Whites have Black friends or Black people in their lives (Bonilla-Silva, 2006). Whites, also for the most part, live primarily in all White neighborhoods, largely due to rampant racial housing segregation (Massey & Denton, 1993). "Residential segregation is not a neutral fact. It systematically undermines the social and economic well being of Blacks in the United States" (Massey & Denton, 1993, p. 104). It is interesting to note that 79% of the teachers surveyed live outside of the district. Even more revealing is that none of the five participating teachers live in the dominantly all Black neighborhood of the school. It is of further interest to note that the five participating teachers all grew up in all-White towns nearby. Thus, living outside the school neighborhood and growing up in all-White suburbs will probably affect attitudes on race.

How does color-blind discourse directly impact an identified non-school ready Black child? First of all, the White teacher's perceptions and views on race, as Ms. Smith states, that they do not see it as a factor in schooling, is dismissive and deficit-based. For example, all of Ms. Moore's late registrants, who are identified as non-school ready, including Derek, are Black. She does not think that Derek's race has anything to do with his identification of low performance. She is not even factoring in the fact that his family does not speak English and has immigrated from a very poor Black nation (Haiti). Ms. Smith expects Billy, who has never gone to formal schooling before, to immediately adapt to the school culture (White middle class normative culture) and believes that his brown skin is not a factor. She, as do the others, believe that it is the parents' commitment to education that directly affects the child's schooling progress. Yet, there is a plethora of research that reveals that race is a factor in early childhood education, and that being Black, specifically, is a hindrance in schooling. For example, according to The Office of Civil Rights, 1.1 million of the overall 2.8 million suspensions are of Black young children (US Department of Education, 2013/2014 report). Harry and Klinger found that up to 30 to 50% of a White teacher's classes (in predominately Black schools) are referred to the special education team (Harry & Klingner, 2006). These research figures conclude that the race of the child does matter and will affect their schooling trajectory.

The third identified race ideology is Race Cognizant. This is what Frankenberg would describe as the awareness of inherent structural differences in race that lead to inequalities within American society (Frankenberg, 1993). This means that Whites, teachers or otherwise, are aware and critically active in the pursuit of racial equality within the framework of the United States school system.

Ironically, this is the ideology that the early childhood teachers in this study believe they relate to. However, as stated earlier, they are in some ways still perpetuating color evasion/color-blind discourse, which means that they are not completely aware of the overall inherent racist societal structures that influence schooling.

If these early childhood educators did actually fall into this category of race ideology, I believe it would deeply impact the school lives of the identified non-school ready Black child. For example, if Ms. Watson becomes more aware of the inherent racist societal structures that impact schooling, she may be more understanding of Michael's absences. Instead she needs to be critiquing the school system and how it forces a young Black child to adapt to a foreign culture. This could help her to understand why Michael feels it is necessary to lie to her about his absences so that he can protect his family. Also, if Ms. Franklin could see the positives of Lina's daycare experience, instead of negating it in its entirety, then the parents may feel more comfortable within the new system.

White Discomfort

Research shows that Whites in general are not used to thinking about themselves as racial identities (Frankenberg, 1993; Leonardo, 2013; Randolph, 2013). Thus, the discomfort that the teachers in this study display when referring to a child's race and how it might or might not be related to the identification of school readiness follows this trend. Their discomfort around the topic of race is in itself the product of the color-blind discourse in the school district and the community at large. When I ask Ms. Franklin about race and how it may be a factor in the status/identification of *school readiness*, she states:

> That's a tough question . . . uh . . . that's a tough one . . . I don't know . . . I have to think about that. I just can't answer one second later.

Earlier in this same interview, Ms. Franklin reveals her discomfort with the issue of her being White and Lina and her parents being Black. The following is an excerpt from this interview:

Ms. Franklin: They (Lina's parents) are not really behind me . . . I am not used to that. . . . All of my parents . . . usually I develop a relationship with them.

Me:	Do you think it has to do with the fact that she is taken out for AI? (Academic Intervention)
Ms. Franklin:	Yes . . . and . . . I . . . I . . . I think it is a bit of a racial issue.
Me:	Did they say that to you?
Ms. Franklin:	They did not say that to me . . . but they said it to another parent who told me.
Me:	And did you talk to them about this?
Ms. Franklin:	No . . . I . . . I didn't talk to them straight forward about it but I talked to them about how . . . I felt they were just worried about her . . . and I said . . . just because you go to AI doesn't mean . . . it's just extra help. . . . Why wouldn't they want that?
Me:	They didn't want her to be labeled? Or something?
Ms. Franklin:	Yeah . . . I think they thought she was classified.

The above is an example of race avoidance on the part of Ms. Franklin. Clearly, she is upset that parents might think that she is insensitive to matters involving race in her own classroom. She builds trusting relationships with her parents and is confused by Lina's parents' hostile response toward her. She feels uncomfortable broaching the matter directly with the parents, so instead tries to address surrounding concerns. She is uncomfortable with this discussion and almost doesn't even want to bring it up. It is interesting to note that there is more hesitancy in speech during discussions with participating teachers about race.

White discomfort also stems from White fragility, which means that Whites have trouble even discussing the topic for fear of being labeled racist. They are so used to their White privilege that they do not want to believe that racism actually exists. Diangelo writes about this phenomenon in her book *What does it mean to be White? Developing White racial literacy.* White people suffer from racial illiteracy, and therefore do not know how to talk about race (Diangelo, 2012). It is not uncommon for a White person to feel or react in a fragile manner when trying to discuss their own White privilege. They do not want to be reminded that they are benefitting from the racist structure of American society. Thus, they pretend it does not exist and try to avoid discussions about race or racial relationships.

Talking about race and the discomfort with this topic may stem from the fact that there are a majority of White middle class K/1 teachers (51 out of 54) in this district. The majority of the children at Grayson are Black (differing populations), and as such these teachers have at least fifteen out of twenty-three children that are non-White in their rooms. Only one teacher, Ms. Moore, talks about this as an issue. The youngest of the participating teachers (age 27), she responds to a comment in the focus group acknowledging that she is the only teacher that identifies differences in the Black populations in her classroom. She does not want to generalize about her specific Black populations, but instead recognizes differences in culture. She states:

> My honest thoughts . . . I have a lot of problems . . . not problems . . . I notice a lot with the Haitian children that there is a difference in language. . . . I am speaking English. . . . You are speaking Creole . . . it's a cultural difference and maybe he (Derek) can understand me clearly . . . but maybe he is not talking to anyone at home . . . in his own language . . . lots of times it's hard for me to connect with him. . . . Then I see African American children and then I see the children . . . maybe first generation African . . . Nigeria . . . Kenya . . . mostly what I see is the African American parents don't really show up for things . . . they are not always helping at home . . .

She does not lump all of her Black students together and seems to be aware of variations in cultural expectations. Yet, it must be noted that she is also reinforcing stereotypes about various Black cultures. In the focus group, she is clearly nervous that she is the only one who speaks about differences in Black populations. When I point it out, she says, "That makes me sweaty!" Ms. Franklin then says, "You are the only one." And Ms. Moore responds with, "It is just an observation." It is almost as if she is sorry she has brought it up at all.

In her research, Randolph (2013) interviews White and Black teachers on the topic of race, multiculturalism and color-blind discourse. She notices that most of the White teachers in her study assume that Black children in their classrooms are African American (Randolph, 2013). She believes this is crucial to the continued White discomfort of these White teachers, as they are not even aware of the differing Black populations in their room.

> The assumption that Black means African American is common in most major Eastern cities, except for New York (and possibly New Jersey), where teachers have more awareness of Black ethnic diversity.
>
> (Randolph, 2013, p. 19)

This means that in general Randolph finds that White teachers are not able to differentiate between different Black populations. Ironically, my research takes place in the New York tri-state area, where White teachers are cited as supposedly being more aware of different Black populations.

During my research, I notice that there are times when the teacher participants are confused about the Black populations in their classrooms. Many teachers have trouble identifying the background culture of the Black children. The following is an excerpt from an interview with Ms. Smith (Billy's teacher). I am asking her about the children, including Billy, that are being pulled out for Academic Intervention.

Me: Are they all Black?

Ms. Smith: Three.

Me:	Three out of five?
Ms. Smith:	There was four . . . so three out of four.
Me:	I am sorry . . . so Black children are the majority?
Ms. Smith:	mmmmmhmmmm
Me:	And there is one White kid? Is that what you are saying?
Ms. Smith:	Yes . . . and the education of the parent.
Me:	Of the parent?
Ms. Smith:	Yeah.
Me:	Explain?
Ms. Smith:	One of the children . . . the parents have a higher education . . . the other three . . . the three of them . . .
Me:	Did they graduate high school?
Ms. Smith:	I don't know . . . that I don't know . . . I know they speak another language . . . but I know the other family so I know . . . but the other three families. . . . One I know speaks another language and the other two have accents . . . so clearly they do speak another language . . .
Me:	Where are they from?
Ms. Smith:	I want to say . . . two are from Haiti and where is the other little guy from? Oh this is terrible . . . I can't remember but it's not Haiti . . . it's not . . .
Me:	Is it Africa?
Ms. Smith:	I don't think so.
Me:	Okay.
Ms. Smith:	And he mentioned it but I can't think of it.

It clearly bothers Ms. Smith that she can't identify the country of origin of the Black child in question. She is also unsure which of the families speak another language at home or just have accents. She is perplexed by the origin of these accents because there is a large population of Haitian children at Grayson, so she believes that they might be from there.

Randolph claims that there is recognition of the different ethnic groups of Whites (and also Latinos to some degree) but not of the varied diverse populations of Blacks. The native White comes first in the hierarchal structure, then White immigrant, Asian immigrants, Latino immigrants and finally Blacks (native or immigrant). Therefore, she concludes that Blacks, whether voluntary or involuntary immigrants, are the lowest in the schooling hierarchal structure and as such are further marginalized (Randolph, 2013). Randolph maintains that the teachers in her research (in a large midwest city) value ethnicity more than skin color, and therefore a Black child is perceived as more deficient (Randolph, 2013).

This means that Derek, who is a Haitian Black, is treated the same as Michael, who is African American. Ethnicity or differences in Black populations do not make a difference to the White teacher. Instead, the teachers in this study are aware of the White ethnicities in their classrooms, such as:

Italian, Irish, Jewish and etc. This, in turn, means that they will read more stories/books that culturally respond to these White ethnicities in their classroom, rather than read diverse books on different Black populations.

Race and Meritocracy

Ms. Watson, Michael's kindergarten teacher, believes that any child regardless of race or socio-economic class can rise up and overcome their circumstances and do well in school. When I ask her whether race is a factor in the identification of non-school ready children, she states:

> No, I mean . . . I shouldn't say no . . . I am sure it (race) does . . . but again there are shades of gray but I have one child who comes from a single mom household . . . strong family values . . . couldn't afford preschool . . . but the mom is working with him and he's my top reader . . . he's my top mathematician He's my top . . . and he's Black and he's male and he's doing great.

According to her, this child is an example of how all children, regardless of where they come from, can succeed from hard work. She uses this particular example when discussing race as a factor in *school readiness* identification because it proves to her that it is not about the child's skin color/tone but instead it is based on effort. However, this is her exception. There is only one Black child in her class that fits this meritocratic example. Ms. Watson contends that this is only because of the hard work and effort from his single parent mom. This discourse, based on meritocracy, continues to perpetuate a color-blind discourse because the child's skin color has nothing to do with the child's success or lack of success in school. This thought process, again, does not take into account that the school system is a part of a larger racist societal structure.

It is also important to note here that Ms. Watson is aware of Black boy stereotypes. Ferguson critically analyzes these stereotypes in the hopes to clarify and make others (White teachers) aware of labeling Black boys in deficit constructs. In chapter one, "Don't believe the hype," she explicitly confronts these given stereotypes and myths about Black boys (Ferguson, 2001). "Suspensions disproportionately involved African American males," she states in her research, citing Oakland schools, where 28% of the population is Black boys, but they comprise 53% of all school suspensions (Ferguson, 2001, p. 3).

Being a boy in itself is cause for concern for a teacher, as most punishments, isolating activities and referrals to the special education team are boys (Ferguson, 2001; Harry & Klingner, 2006). Boys are more likely to be considered 'troublemakers' or 'non-listeners' (i.e., Derek, Billy and Jay). Boys will be boys is the old adage, and this myth may be still viewed as reality, as boys are cited as more aggressive and are less able to sit than young girls in the early childhood classroom (Ferguson, 2001; US Department of Education, 2013–14). It is important to note that four out of the five children identified and picked to be a part of this study are boys, and when speaking to the teachers, the majority of all of their academically and socially low children are boys. Therefore, the myth of the Black boy is a double whammy and hard to escape.

Ms. Watson clearly believes that this one particular Black boy defies these mythical odds, and in spite of being Black and poor, he is able to exceed the school's expectations, largely because of the hard-working parent. Thus, this argument of meritocracy, and the ability of all American children to be on the same level playing field, reinforces everyday color-blind discourse. Wolfmeyer, a notable critical math educator, states, "Such an ideal describes a society where individuals in positions of power, authority and wealth achieved their status as a result of merits they have attained" (Wolfmeyer, forthcoming in 2017, pages not set). According to him, teachers adhering to this theory are just promoting White supremacy and reproducing classist structures (Wolfmeyer, forthcoming 2017).

If this young low-income Black child that Ms. Watson refers to can be at the top of her kindergarten class, then all Black children can do the same. Yet, why is Michael toward the bottom of her class? And then why is it that Ms. Springstein's seven lowest children are all Black, including Jay? Why is it that the majority of this school's population in Academic Intervention or referred to the special education team are all Black?

It is important to note that large populations of Black children (mostly boys) are classified and referred to special education (Harry & Klinger, 2006), while others are constantly being suspended and systemically punished within the school system (Ferguson, 2001; US Department of education, 2013–14). In Ferguson's study school, 70% of all the children punished in house or suspended were Black boys (Ferguson, 2001). As stated above, statistics and raw data just do not support this meritocratic theory, especially when it comes to young Black boys.

Ms. Franklin believes that she weighs in differently on this issue of meritocracy. She states, "It is not a level playing field." In one of her interviews, she makes it clear that she has to provide more schema for low-income Black children in order for them to catch up with the rest of the children (i.e., White children).

> A lot of these children come here without life experience . . . no schema . . . very little schema because they haven't gone anywhere or seen anything. I think the Smartboard has helped these kids . . . with their nonfiction reading and has given them a lot of schema. I think the next best thing to being there is actually taking these virtual tours and it is wonderful.

According to her, Black children start at a deficit by lacking schema (background knowledge), and therefore she has to help them to acquire more schema in order to catch up with the average student. This notion extends the meritocracy argument because, once again, hard work pays off. And in this case it is overcoming the deficit of background knowledge (schema).

This refers to another section in this book in which Ms. Franklin relates all important values/knowledge systems as the same, middle class values. Here she is critical of the Black child's lack of knowledge/schema related to Western middle class values/traditions. She is ultimately saying that a child that has never been exposed to certain places (i.e., museums) or ideas is deficient. But what if this is not the case? Perhaps she should look at the strengths of each child, and what specific schema they bring to the classroom, instead of what they are lacking. Clearly, Lina lacks schema, according to Ms. Franklin. In actuality, Lina has her own cultural schema, one that may not be in line with the normative structures of the White middle class school system. By practicing Funds of Knowledge, Lina's teacher would be embracing other value systems/cultures, instead of looking for deficits.

I must be clear that the word 'schema' is a normative schooling term that is overused in regards to identification with *school readiness*. Lack of schema is more commonly referred to when speaking about a low-income Black child than a White middle class child. Why is this? The word itself is part of the problem. Schema is defined as prior knowledge that helps to further new understandings. Simply put, if a child knows that pastrami is a type of meat, they will understand the context in a story. As a teacher in an all Black and Latino school, a question involving pastrami came up on a standardized test and all of the children in my classroom got the question wrong because they had never heard of a pastrami sandwich before. Schema therefore give some children an advantage over others when involved in a new learning experience. The understanding and belief in this concept in itself just perpetuates the marginalization of the low-income non-White student. Their prior knowledge/schema is not as important. For example, Derek's knowledge of his Haitian culture will not help him on his future third grade standardized test, because tests and academic core requirements are based on White middle class knowledge systems.

Michael Apple refers to this concept as "official knowledge." According to Apple, there is no such thing as neutral knowledge. Therefore all knowledge utilized in the American school system is based on the dominant logic of knowledge and what a specific set of people (curriculum writers, textbook and test creators) believes is the proper set of knowledges to acquire. There is a hierarchy of knowledge systems and the dominant system, based on White middle class discourse, is the prevailing set of knowledges utilized and valued within the school system (Apple, 1993, 2001).

Today the official knowledge system is the Common Core. As I explained earlier, this set of knowledges has been created by the neoliberal educational agenda to further privatize and regulate public schools. Big corporations, such as Pearson, are a large part of this knowledge set and their agenda is to profit from the Common Core and standardized testing. This official knowledge system, like all others in the past, does not respond to or relate to low-income Black populations. In other words, the creators of this official knowledge system are not low-income Blacks and also do not have any understanding of different Black populations in the American school system.

Issues of Race and Socio-Economic Status

Institutional racism and poverty co-exist in America and therefore must have strong compounded effects on the schooling experience of low-income Black children. If Black families suffer job discrimination, low wages, housing discrimination and other forms of institutional racism, it is bound to directly affect a young Black child's *school readiness* status. In Anyon's research findings, she reveals that true educational reform can't occur without critically examining the macroeconomic inequities within the school community itself. Low wages of Black parents affect their child's schooling experience, and Blacks, overall, earn less than Whites, even in minimum wage jobs (Anyon, 2005). Residential segregation and unfair housing practices, such as red-lining (steering Blacks into one neighborhood), also affect the everyday lives of young Black children in school. Lack of health insurance and poor overall health conditions also affect the low-income Black community. Anyon states:

> Being poor in a rich country can lead to ill-placed shame, pervasive despair, and anger. Living in poverty is to experience daily crises of food, a place to live and ways to keep your children safe.
>
> (Anyon, 2005, p. 61)

At Grayson there are large numbers of Black children that qualify for free/reduced lunch (43% of the overall population of the school), and they come in some mornings very hungry, complaining of stomachaches and headaches. Hungry children have trouble focusing and attending to their work. Teachers have snacks on hand so that they can provide food over the course of the day to those who need it. Being from a low-income household can mean a lack of food, and this could directly impact a child's *school readiness* status.

Jay is always hungry. He comes into school hungry, as he usually misses the free breakfast, and leaves hungry. He eats really slowly, and doesn't usually have the time to finish all of his lunch in the given twenty minute lunchtime slot. This means he comes back to class still hungry from lunch. The kindergarten classroom he is in doesn't always have snack time. Ms. Springstein says there just isn't enough time in her schedule (see time compression). Being hungry means it is harder for him to concentrate and focus on his schoolwork. And since he is very active, he needs even more food and hydration.

Derek and Billy are also very active and qualify for free breakfast and lunch as well. Again, if they come in late, due to their parents' work schedules, they miss their opportunity for a school breakfast, which usually means they have nothing to eat all morning. Derek, as a kindergartner, has the last lunch slot and eats around 1:25pm, which is very late in the day, especially if he has no time for breakfast. They constantly complain of being hungry, and their teachers have to give them a countdown to lunch in order to quell them.

Billy's hand is up in the air. Ms. Smith doesn't notice him quickly enough so he shouts out,
"How many minutes until lunch???"
Ms. Smith ignores him and makes a face. But now the class is interested, so a White boy raises his hand and waits patiently for Ms. Smith to call on him.
Meanwhile, Billy says again,
"When's lunch?"
Ms. Smith is visibly annoyed and says,
"Please do not call out in this classroom."
After a beat she goes on with her writing lesson but the White boy's hand is still up.
"Yes, _____," she finally says to him.
"How many minutes until lunch, Ms. Smith?" he asks.
Others nod eagerly awaiting her answer. She sighs and looks at me and then at the clock on the wall.
"About twenty minutes, but we have a lot to do, so no more interruptions please!"
Billy smiles, as he has his answer, and he seems pleased that lunch is soon.

The combination of being Black and low-income is extremely hard in an early childhood program, because they both work in tandem outside the mainstream normative discourse of White and middle class. A middle class Black child has more opportunities to excel in the schooling process, because of their shared middle class values. This is not to say that their race, in itself, does not play a role in how teachers perceive him/her in the classroom, because it does to some extent, but being Black and poor is much harder on a child. It is important to note here that there are only a few Black middle class families at Grayson, and since the total Black population is 44%, then the majority fit this deficit-based category of Black and low-income.

In summary, the 'tough question on race' is embedded into perceptions and identifications of *school readiness*. Differing discourses on race, including: race ideologies, White teacher discomfort, race and the theory of meritocracy and race and issues of socio-economic status, all play a role in how early childhood educators (who are 85% White women) perceive and identify non-school ready children. This, in turn, directly impacts identified low-income Black non-school ready children because then they are essentially relegated to this status due to their race and socio-economic status. The combination of being poor and Black is too much for a young child to overcome in their schooling identification and therefore must be critically analyzed and thought about before White teachers make deficit-based judgments.

Lina, Jay, Derek, Billy and Michael are all low-income and Black. They come from different Black cultures but are viewed as the same in the eyes of their teachers. They are lumped together as the identified non-school ready child who happens to be Black, with assumptions that all Blacks come from the same cultural background. Their teachers are uncomfortable talking about race and reveal their color-blind discourse when asked about the subject. This 'tough question' about race zeros in on their own White fragility and discomfort. It all relates back to the child's parents, and their lack of valuing education. Parental blame takes the place of critically reflecting on their own biases/assumptions. The teachers only focus on what these young Black children are lacking (schema based on White middle class values) instead of embracing and celebrating their own specific cultural backgrounds. They may say 'race is not a factor,' and yet it is the key factor in the identification and schooling trajectory of all five children in question.

7 Inequities and Inequalities in Early Childhood Education Programs

In a true working democracy, providing equal access to quality early childhood education programs is essential. The present two-tiered preschool model, of middle and upper class children receiving high quality preschool versus the poor quality or no preschool program available for the low-income/poor child, needs to be eliminated. The goal is to challenge all deficit discourses, including *school readiness*, and work toward equity in early childhood programs nation-wide.

School reform of any kind, including the inherent issues related to *school readiness* status, must be first addressed on the macroeconomic level. Anyon, a noted educational policy expert/researcher, calls for a national movement on school reform that centers on bridging societal inequalities and inequities (Anyon, 2005). Thus, future early childhood policy that involves real reform has to be designed within the framework of challenging and reforming the societal structures that are inherently racist and class biased.

In this chapter I will examine Grayson's school district and utilize it as an example of the American society as a whole and the structural inequities and inequalities that affect the schooling process and deficit identification of the individual low-income Black child. As noted earlier, there are five different elementary schools, yet the two schools physically closest to the nearby urban metropolis have the highest populations of low-income non-White children. Thus, Grayson experiences both inequities and inequalities within the greater district and within society at large.

Inequities

Inequities between school districts and even within school districts are of paramount concern. Anyon states, "Money matters" (Anyon, 2005, p. 47), and it is the key to the inequities in our public school system. Where you live specifically accounts for the quality of your neighborhood school. Residing in a poor economic area, with lower property taxes, directly affects the quality of the schools. Districts that spend less per student, due to taxes, offer less services and resources. Thus, gaps in funding are an ever-present problem. For example, in New York, the schools with the highest minority school districts receive over $2,000 less per student than the districts with high percentages of White children (Anyon, 2005).

Grayson, located in the only low-income Black area in the township, has a large population of low-income non-White children, and all of the children in this study live within a seven-block radius. Many of these children are from immigrant families where English is not the first language of the household. In order to keep the school desegregated, the district has to bus in White middle class children from the other side of town. This is the only school in the district that a family can opt into; otherwise families are zoned to attend their neighborhood school. This means that another school in the district has only 6% reduced or free lunch families in their school as opposed to a much higher 43% at Grayson. This leads to inherent inequities in school funding, as families in the 6% school have much more money.

One of the main support systems for acquiring funds in a local school is the PTO (parent–teacher organization). Schools with families that earn higher incomes can raise more funds on a regular basis. Therefore, even though the school district gives a similar amount of funds to each school, all schools do not have the same amount of funds at the end of the day.

Schools with high-powered PTOs, such as in the other four district elementary schools, are able to raise funds at a quicker rate. They host galas, dinners, auctions, bake sales, selling coupon books and etc. in order to raise funds from the families in their school. Schools like Grayson, however, struggle with fundraisers, as the majority of their families (like Jay's and the others) are working several jobs to make ends meet and do not have any funds left over for donations. An example of this fundraising inequity relates to another school I taught at in an urban district nearby. In this public school, there is a huge flea market held every Saturday morning. The venders, local artisans and vintage antique dealers rent out the school playground space to hold this flea market. It's hugely popular in this gentrifying neighborhood and earns the school PTO up to $100,000 per year. This money helps the school buy extra technological equipment, school trips and other resources that schools within two miles away cannot provide.

Several articles in the *Boston Globe* and *Chicago Tribune* have specifically investigated this inequity of funding by differing PTOs. In one instance, in a suburb of Boston, the school district has to step in and stop certain schools with large fundraising campaigns from purchasing more technology and instead makes them utilize the funds for other items. Other schools in this same district, with little PTO fundraising, have for years been unable to purchase technology systems that these schools are providing, and the parents are complaining that it is not fair. After a thorough investigation, it's discovered that during the previous five years, anonymous donations were being given to a specific school, which gave them the opportunity to spend over $167,000 on new technology for their school, whereas another school in this same district raised $0 for technology (Boston Globe.com, 2014).

The difference in technological equipment is a good example of this inherent inequity in funding in this particular school district. In a school in the wealthier section of town, the PTO raises enough funds to get ipads for each kindergarten student. They also raise money for Smartboards, laptops and document cameras. When you walk into this school, every classroom, grades kindergarten through second, is equipped with all of the above technological tools. Just a mile or two away, Grayson has very little technological equipment. In grades K-2 there are only four classrooms that have working Smartboards, and there is one ipad cart for all the grades to share. Recently, Grayson has purchased Google chromebook carts, but again only to share on each floor (ten classrooms). In my classroom as a first grade teacher at Grayson, I have accumulated five ipads in over five years, which is not as helpful in a classroom of up to twenty-two students. Also, I have never had a Smartboard, use of a document camera or any laptops. Ironically, my children do not have this technology at home either, and therefore especially need more support at school.

When the district purchases a computer program, there is talk that low-income families in the district (at Grayson) may receive free Kindle Fire tablets. In order for this new program (ST MATH) to work effectively and help students achieve higher scores on the standardized math test, the district believes each child should be practicing the program at home for at least five to ten hours per week. This, they know, may be hard for the low-income child (at Grayson), as they don't have access to the technology at home. Before they buy hundreds of Kindle Fire tablets, they circulate a home technology survey. Teachers have to give out this survey at back to school night and then collect them for the district. Interestingly, most of the surveys reveal that these families do have access to technology at home, which is not necessarily the case. Jay's family, for example, say they have access to a computer at home, however, there's only one computer for the whole family to use, and the internet service is spotty at best. This gave Jay very little individual time to utilize the computer, so he does not get to practice ST MATH at home. Other families reveal to me that they have to use the computer for work and therefore the child has no time on it. In any case, they have limited access to technology. After collecting this survey from Grayson, the district concludes that there are enough computers/tablets in the homes of the low-income students, and so they cancel the order of Kindle Fire tablets. Therefore, even in this case, where the district thinks it's being inclusive by asking about home technology access, they end up doing nothing to help these low-income families with the application of this mandatory district-wide program.

Meanwhile, the other schools in the district have families with four to six technological systems to utilize ST MATH. They have homes with multiple laptops, iPads, iPhones, desktops and tablets. This means that these children can practice ST MATH for five to ten hours a week, which later helps them (according to the district analysis of the program) achieve higher test scores.

Table 7.1 Grayson vs. the other Elementary Schools in the District

	Grayson	#1	#2	#3	#4
Auto-document camera in each classroom K-2	No	Yes	Yes	Yes	Yes
ipads for each student	No	Yes	Yes	Yes	Yes
Technology in library	No	Yes	Yes	Yes	Yes
Smartboards in every room	No	Yes	Yes	Yes	Yes
Paras in every kindergarten	No	Yes	Yes	Yes	No
5 books or more in class per student	No	Yes	Yes	Yes	No
Lofts or art areas in room	No	Yes	Yes	Yes	No
Ample closets in room	No	Yes	Yes	Yes	No
Sinks in room	Some	All	All	All	Some

*Numbers 1, 2 and 3 are schools with high populations of White middle class children. Number 4 is the other border school with less White middle class children.

Thus, adding this technological program to the district curriculum further exacerbates the educational gap between White middle class children and low-income Black children. In this case, inequities in technological equipment directly affect the upcoming scores on the math standardized test. This example reveals just how deeply rooted school inequities are and how they work within the system. (See Table 7.1.)

Inequities in school funds are a prime example of how schools with low-income populations do not have equal access to school resources/materials. This inequity is a part of the larger problem of the American school system because it perpetuates a widening of the educational gap between low-income Blacks and middle class Whites. Ultimately, a child (low-income and Black) who is classified as non-school ready does not have the same opportunities to become school ready due to lack of school resources. Thus, it is a no win situation for the identified non-school ready child. They are stuck in their neighborhood school with little to no funds and they do not have the same access to quality in the public education system.

Inequalities

Inequalities differ from inequities and are the reason for inequities in the first place. They are inherent structural differences that lead to one group having an advantage or privilege over the other. In American society, privilege or lack of privilege derives from the racial and economic status of the individual. Therefore, being an individual who is from the background of a low-income family and is Black means that you will suffer inequalities or lack of societal privilege. Gillborn, in his research, concludes that racism, as a structure, is not accidental (Gillborn, 2008). It is a structure that is set up so one group (Whites) can reap benefits and rewards over other populations (non-Whites). It is a power dynamic in which various institutions, such as schools, re-enforce and reproduce daily.

Grayson is the proverbial 'black sheep' of the district. Many of the rooms do not have air conditioning and or proper ventilation, as it is an old building. There is less physical space, as there are portables in the back, and still the classes are overcrowded. There is a problem with procuring enough substitute teachers in this school too, largely because substitutes get to choose which school they want to work in, and very few (only Black and other non-White substitutes) will come to substitute for teachers at Grayson. Some cite personal safety as a factor. This, of course will not change, as these substitutes are paid the same amount if they go to work at Grayson for the day or at any other of the schools in the district. This leads to real problems for the teachers and the students at Grayson.

One issue is that Grayson teachers can't always go to district-wide professional development workshops, because even though they have booked a substitute weeks in advance, the substitutes have all chosen to work at other schools. This means that teachers can get a call in their car, on the way to the workshop, by administrators telling them that they have no coverage for their classrooms and that they must report to school at once. This does not happen very often in the other schools, as they can usually find someone to come in and cover their classes.

Another issue is with the students. Since substitutes get to choose where they work and do not usually choose Grayson, most of the lower quality substitutes are the only ones available. They sometimes have little or no experience in the classroom and no real classroom management skills. Many times I have come back from being out and had to calm my class down after a rough experience with a substitute who clearly did not know how to teach a first grade class. I recall a specific time where I am selected as an alternate for jury duty and I have to speak to the judge about my concerns of leaving my classroom for up to three weeks with an incompetent substitute and therefore he dismisses me. Also, there have been many times at Grayson when teachers call in sick and there are no substitutes available, so special education teachers or reading teachers get pulled from their normal classroom assignments in order to be a makeshift classroom substitute. This means that the children being serviced by these teachers receive no services for the day.

Still another unequal practice is when lack of substitutes and availability of special education/reading teachers and classes have to be split up and extra children are placed in another classroom for the day. Any given day, there can be too many teachers out to be replaced, so the principal will take a class list and physically drop off three to four children into another classroom for the day. Children, regardless of their grade, are placed in a nearby classroom and are expected to work on their grade level for that day. There are many days when I have kindergarteners and second graders placed in my first grade classroom. This practice is detrimental to student learning and still occurs to this day, even with teacher complaints.

Derek does not like to be placed in other classrooms. He is the kind of child who does very poorly when his beloved Ms. Moore is absent. He does a little better when placed with a teacher he knows, like his reading specialist, but most of the time he has strangers in his classroom and he always gets in trouble. He is usually sent to the principal's office when the substitute can't take anymore or he shadows his reading specialist all day. Billy is the same way. He crumbles when Ms. Smith is out; luckily she is not absent much. Usually he spends his time roaming the halls, prolonging his re-entry into the classroom. He doesn't do well with strangers and will not listen or follow directions. Jay is never absent, because no one is at home during the day to watch him. He tries to behave with the substitute but usually has a hard time controlling his body movement and gets in trouble. Sometimes his reading interventionist will come by and take him for a longer period of time and sometimes he is just ignored all day long. Lina uses the time to try and catch up with projects in class. If the substitute does not have a real plan, she just goes to her work table and tries to complete her work. If the substitute spots her she gets in trouble, but it is worth it because then she has done more on a project and Ms. Franklin will be pleased when she returns. In general, these 'non-school' ready children do not do well with substitutes, especially ones that have no training or understanding of their outside position within the mainstream classroom.

There is a negative stigma attached to this wonderful school and it's largely because it is located in a low-income Black neighborhood, where teachers in other parts of the district do not want to work. At district-wide workshops, it is very clear that these teachers do not respect or understand the differences in populations at Grayson. Each workshop is geared to their populations (mostly White middle class) and does not account for other populations and their possible different needs. In one workshop, related to technology, one of Grayson's teachers asks about her classroom population and how they can implement a new computer-based program (ST MATH) if their children have no technology at home. After the distribution of the technology survey, the district feels that all bases have been covered and now it's up to the family to find a way to utilize technology at home. The flat response from the district math supervisor is, "they can go to the library." This shows that the district itself does not understand or have the ability to understand the needs of Grayson's population or how to cater to these specific needs.

Racism, both structural and personal, is also an issue in this district. Teachers utilize negative word constructs, like "these children" and "you know these families" and don't even realize it. Deficit-based stereotypes also run amok within the district. I have had many teachers, outside of Grayson, approach me and ask me if I have ever been mugged or hurt outside of school. They feel sorry for me and the other teachers working at Grayson and always ask us how we can do it every day. These teachers do not go to this neighborhood, or section of town, so they can only make assumptions based on crime reports they read or hear about. Grayson is deemed to be in the unsafe part of town because it is two blocks away from a large urban center. It must be noted that during the seven years I worked here, I never felt scared or threatened in the neighborhood, and I walked everywhere. It might be because I grew up in New York City, and do not believe that graffiti and people of color make a neighborhood unsafe. Yet, clearly, many of the teachers in this district do hold distinct racist and stereotypical views of Grayson's surrounding neighborhood, and this affects the negative stigma attached to this school.

When people move to this town, real estate professionals clearly tout the best schools and steer people to certain parts of the district. One school, only one mile west of Grayson, but on the other side of a main boulevard that crosses through town, is so popular that it is hard to buy a house in this particular area. The houses that are for sale in this and other areas in town sell quickly. Middle class White families that move to this town are told they don't want to live in the Grayson area, as it is deemed to be an inferior school. Even the most liberal, progressive minded White transplant family does not buy a house in Grayson's immediate neighborhood, but instead buys it across the boulevard where the White middle class section of houses begins. Thus, residential segregation is part of the problem in this town and most every town in the United States. White middle class families will opt in to Grayson for diversity reasons, and yet they still will not live in the immediate neighborhood. This practice of red-lining and self-selecting a residence based on the racial compass of the neighborhood greatly affects local neighborhood schools.

Overall, I am not sure that this blatant inequality in this school district, or others like it, will ever change without a revamping of the macroeconomic structures (including housing) and the racist ideology that permeates the town itself. It is important to note here that this township is considered highly liberal in policy and practice, and the majority of the population has voted for democrats historically.

The Bigger Picture

Grayson is part of a school district that ironically believes it is fully serving all of its population equally. School board meetings and other public gatherings all center on this concept. Therefore, it's a surprise to the school district, when in 2014, a lawsuit is filed against them by the local ACLU and the Office of Civil Rights. This lawsuit is based on the high percentage of Black children suspended and disciplined within the schools and academic placement. The complaint itself alleges that academic tracking and the frequent use of out of school suspensions by the district violate the U.S. Department of Education regulations related to Title VI of the Civil Rights act of 1964, and section 504 of the rehabilitation Act of 1973 (ACLU complaint, 2014). The intention of this complaint was to vindicate the rights of Black and

Hispanic students and students with disabilities in this particular district. There's a special concern for the Black special education student K–12. In this district, there is a disproportionate rate of suspensions of Black children (14.2%) versus White children (2.7%), which was greater than the state average (ACLU complaint, 2014; US Department of Education, 2013–14).

According to the Office of Civil Rights, a Black child in a public preschool is 3.6 times more likely to be suspended from school than a White preschooler (US Department of Education, 2013–14). Proportionately more Blacks are suspended from early childhood programs than all other populations. Blacks are only 19% of the preschool enrollment, but they are 47% of all suspensions (US Department of Education, 2013–14). In K–12, there are 2.8 million children in the public schools that receive one or more out of school suspensions and 1.1 million of these children are Black (US Department of Education, 2013–14). These figures reveal a crisis of great proportions in our school system. Systemic racism is the issue here, and school districts like the one in this study need to be continually investigated for discriminatory practices.

During my time at Grayson, kindergarten and first grade Black boys were being suspended and disciplined often. I always questioned this procedure. Honestly, what can warrant a young Black child to be suspended from school? One Black male child in my class is suspended for spitting on a girl's pants. Another time a Black boy in my class is suspended for not following lock down procedures. Most of the time it's a problem outside the classroom. Black boys are always getting in trouble at recess. Many days I return from lunch and pick up the class and a Black boy or two are missing from the line. Other children inform me about some incident on the playground and then I get a call from the office to send up their books/homework because they are going home due to outside suspensions.

Academic placement refers to the high referrals of Black children to special education environments. I remember at one point we are told, at Grayson, by our principal, that we have to cut down on referrals of Black children, because our numbers are too high and are being scrutinized by the district. First of all, our numbers have to be much higher because of the high populations of Blacks in the school. Furthermore, this makes sense when looking at the average statistic that White teachers refer up to 50% of their all-Black classrooms (Harry & Klingner, 2006). Over 85% of the national teaching workforce is White, and a lot of them, like in Grayson, are working in predominantly non-White environments; therefore the referral rates will always remain high. At Grayson we are not told until later on that this mandate from the district relates to a lawsuit pending against the district. Thus, this pending lawsuit of discriminatory practices is the only reason for this school and the district to look into trying to slow down the referral process. This has a negative side effect, however, as children with real pressing learning disabilities who happen to be Black cannot be referred to the team until after second grade. Yes, the population of young Black children being referred to the team slowed down quite a bit at Grayson, but this new and improved lower percentage of referrals is not necessarily authentic.

This pending lawsuit illustrates a larger problem within our society. A history of racism is embedded into the core of our school system. Even so-called liberal communities are not fully aware of this inherent racist structure that is practiced everyday. If they are not aware, then this practice goes unquestioned. School board members, district officials and family members are all appalled at the development of this lawsuit, mainly because they can not believe that racist discriminatory practices can be found in their own backyard. This is, however, commonplace, as the Office of Civil rights follows up on thousands of complaints yearly and finds many school districts out of compliance.

Inequities and Inequalities and the Non-School Ready Child

Jay, Derek, Lina, Billy and Michael are directly impacted by the inequity of funds and the unequal practices within their school district. They all experience limited resources, including lack of technology, issues of less physical space, higher rates of referral and more possible in-house and out of school suspensions. As individuals they are discriminated against on a daily basis.

Jay is in line to be sent to the team, but because of the backlash from the lawsuit, he will not go any time soon. He has a decoding problem in reading, but he does not have equal access to programs like Lexia (a reading program) that he can utilize on an ipad that may help him with this issue. He is stuck in a crowded portable, because there is not enough physical space for classrooms in the old main building. He is five years old and needs to move around but has to sit at a table designed for four with five other kindergartners. He does not have the same access to the district-wide math computer program (ST MATH) because the teacher has to share the ipad cart with eight other classrooms and it is hard to schedule a class session for her class. The computer lab that Jay goes to once a week has old personal computers that don't always work. The teacher has to put two to three children on a computer and usually still does not have use of enough computers per child. In the library, Jay has a selection of fewer books. There are thousands fewer titles than at a nearby school (#1 on Table 7.1). Jay does not have many books at home, so he tries to get all of his weather books at the school library. The librarian tries to get more books for Jay, but her funds are limited and so are her parent volunteers. She has to run the library, usually by herself, and tend to the classes that come in for library time. Other schools in the district have a plethora of parent volunteers and extra funds to stock the shelves.

Michael does not have a Smartboard or auto document camera in his classroom. The teacher has to utilize the old school method of an overhead projector, which is harder for him to see from the back of the rug. He does not get to interact with the Smartboard like other children his age at nearby schools and therefore is limited to what the teacher can project from textbooks. He loves math, but there are fewer math manipulatives in his classroom. He also has no access to calculators and other tools that he would like to work with. He has limited school trips in his classroom, as it is harder for the teachers to raise money for buses. He can't explore other places in the world, without a computer in his classroom. Again he has limited access to the ipad cart and the floating chrome book cart, but is the kind of child who really loves to do his work on the computer. He is soft-spoken and reserved and sometimes just wants to work by himself. He loves the mandated once a week ST MATH computer time and looks forward to it all week, yet other children in the district have access to this program all day long on their individual ipads in their desks or cubbies.

Lina is stuck in a hot classroom with no air conditioning. She gets thirsty all the time and there is no water fountain in the room. She knows that Ms. Franklin will not let her out of the room that often, so she drinks more on her way to Academic Intervention. There is no girl's bathroom on her floor, so she has to go either upstairs (with the big kids) or downstairs by the lunchroom. This is also a time for her to get more water and she looks forward to it. The carpeting in the hallways is old and frayed in places, so she trips sometimes. She has a hard time navigating the carpet and the stairs. In the classroom there is no sink, so they don't paint as much. She likes to paint too. The rooms need to be repainted and she sees mice droppings behind the bookshelves. She doesn't really like sitting on the rug, because it doesn't seem that clean, so she rocks back and forth a lot. She is also out of the room a lot getting extra services/support, so sometimes she comes into the room and has no idea what is going on. She misses a lot of class instruction time too, and has a hard time catching up.

Derek is also stuck in a small portable outside. His classroom shares a thin wall with Jay's classroom and he can hear every sound coming from Jay's room. Sometimes there is just too much noise coming from the other side of the wall and he has to clasp his hands over his ears. He has limited space to move around and usually circles the room many times in the day. He would rather be outside on the playground with wide open spaces but is confined to his small portable for six hours a day. He loves listening to Ms. Moore read out loud, but there are very few books displayed in the room that he can look at. He has no English books at home and only gets to see a limited selection of books at the school library once a week. He has been suspended once already and he is only in kindergarten. He gets suspended two more times in the first few months of first grade. He is labeled a trouble-maker and a behavior problem early on.

Billy is lucky, he is one of the few children in the school that has a Smartboard in his room, but it has been broken for a while. Ms. Smith put in a request to fix it, as it is an older Smartboard, but the district technicians haven't come yet. She wrote a grant for it many years ago and got it after much effort, but now it doesn't always work right. She is planning to write another local grant for five ipads this year so she can have a total of ten ipads in the room, a treat. Billy likes to write on the computer, but there is no computer in the room, so he waits for computer lab, which is once a week. He doesn't like to write long-hand and usually dawdles with his pencil instead. Billy has also been suspended for behavior issues and has spent a half-day in the principal's office. He could not receive an out of school suspension because no one was home to look after him. Like Lina, his classroom is very hot. He is usually sweaty and he is constantly wiping his brow. There is a standing fan, but all it does is blow hot air around the room. Luckily the teacher lets him keep a water bottle on his desk, but he still wants to leave the room as much as possible to put cold water on his face.

All five of these children represent other children nation-wide that do not have the same access to educational resources, materials and services. It is not a coincidence that these inherent inequities and inequalities are dominantly displayed in this primarily low-income Black neighborhood. As long as there are monetary inequities and racist structural actions (like red-lining), young low-income Black children, like Lina, Billy, Derek, Michael and Jay, will directly suffer from these inequities and inequalities within their schools.

In conclusion, inequities and inequalities exist within school districts as well as school district to school district. There will be more identified non-school ready children in these schools, mainly because they tend to serve low-income non-White populations. These children have less access to resources, books, technology and appropriate classroom spaces than White children at other schools in the same district. A lawsuit filed by the ACLU and the Office of Civil Rights is still pending within this district, which reveals deeper issues of inequality and inequities. Several of the boys in the study have already been suspended multiple times, thus adding to the high rates of suspensions of Black children in the district. The five young Black children are directly affected by these severe discrepancies within their everyday schooling experience.

In order for this ongoing systemic problem of inequities and unequal practices to be challenged, nation-wide policies and structures must change. In the next chapter, a call for action regarding all of the inherent problems related to the identification and classification of non-school ready children is explored.

8 A Call for Action

Where Are They Now?

It is two years later. I have captured small moments of time in these five children's lives, but what has happened to them? I want to give a thorough update on each child in this study so that the reader understands what usually becomes of a child who is classified as non-school ready.

Lina is still attending Grayson and is just finishing third grade at this writing. She spends her second grade year with the same teacher, Ms. Franklin, in a multi-age classroom (1/2). She continues to receive academic intervention services all throughout second grade. There are no more official interventions, but the parents continue to meet with Ms. Franklin and continually refuse special education testing. Recently, I ask Ms. Franklin about Lina and how she fared in second grade with her and she looks confused. "Was she in second grade with me . . . I don't remember." She thinks about it for a while and then realizes that Lina has stayed with her two years and that she just forgot about her because that year she had several overt behavior problems. When I ask her about her reading, she says that Lina has caught up, although just barely. She does say that the third grade inclusion teacher complains about Lina to her on a regular basis. This is a habit of many teachers at Grayson, and perhaps nation-wide. The new teacher seeks out the old teacher of a child who is identified as non-school ready or exhibits behavior issues in order to complain about that person being placed in their class. It's important to note here that this sometimes happens when the child does well in your class as well.

In third grade, Lina still receives academic intervention, but there are fewer parent meetings now. The parents have remained strong throughout the past three years and have refused special education testing. They clearly want her to stay in regular education as long as she can. She is, however, in a third grade inclusion classroom, where there is a second special education teacher. According to Ms. Franklin, she should stay in inclusion for as long as she can, possibly through fifth grade, as Grayson has one inclusion class per grade. Yet, there is no guarantee that she will be placed in it again in fourth or fifth grade, as she has no IEP (individual education plan) or special education services.

Since Lina's parents are strong advocates, she may make it through the system without special education testing, and she also may continue to flounder academically. Being at the bottom of a regular education or inclusion classroom is hard on a child. Insecurities run deep and the child feels each failure daily. Lina would probably do better in a smaller classroom, like in a private school, where her individual needs could be met on an ongoing basis, yet her parents do not have the funds for the high price of private schools, so it may never happen. She would also excel in a home school environment, but both her parents work, so that is also not a real option. Hopefully, she will not get lost in this system, and won't drop out or become disillusioned with school and her academic talents. She may continue to be tracked into low-level academic placements. It's hard to say, as she has already been labeled in such a deficit way at a young age.

Billy left Grayson after his first grade year. Ms. Smith is told that his mom has moved again to another school district due to a divorce and therefore Billy attends a new school in second grade. Ms. Smith recommends he be retained, due to lack of social maturity and being behind in all academic areas. It is not clear what happened at the new district, but it is likely he did not get retained but struggled in second grade as well. The mother has a pattern of moving annually in order to procure jobs to support her family, thus it is probable that Billy is in another school for third grade during this past year. It is also likely that he either got retained once or has been tested for special education services.

When I speak to Ms. Smith, she says she will look into what happened to Billy, but she never gets back to me. She does know that the divorce his parents were going through was hard on Billy and it affected him at the end of the year, as his father moved back to Western Africa. She also told me that he was not retained in the new school district, but never heard from his new teacher, even after she reached out to her.

Derek moves up to first grade at Grayson but it does not go well. After being with a kindergarten teacher that adores him and gives him the extra attention he needs, he is placed in a first grade classroom with a teacher who is distant and labels him a troublemaker. He gets into trouble regularly, is suspended twice during his short stay and by December of that year is transferred to the ELL program at another district school. If you remember he tested for the ELL program in the beginning of his kindergarten year but his mom could not accommodate the transfer due to her work schedule and bus drop off times. The mother must have rallied her extended kinship network to get someone to pick him up at the bus on time.

Last year (in his first grade year), Derek appears at Ms. Moore's kindergarten classroom door. He is knocking wildly trying to get her attention, as she is already starting her teaching day. When she comes to the door he is all by himself. A cousin has brought him to the wrong classroom, but he is smiling. She laughs as she tells me this story because it has made her day, seeing him on her doorstep like old times. Clearly, when he thinks of his classroom and his teacher, he still thinks of Ms. Moore. He doesn't want to let her go. She calls the office and a secretary comes out to escort him to his first grade classroom (before he leaves for the ELL program at the other school). Ms. Moore has not heard about him since this time. She is still worried about him, and hopes that he is doing better at this other school.

If Derek ever tests out of ELL, he will most probably head back to Grayson, and without a caring teacher, he will get into trouble regularly. Middle school will only be worse for him, as there are fewer services and more children. There are also fewer school counselors, which is important for a child like Derek. He needs to be adored, heard and patted on his shoulder and have a deep connection to his teacher, just like he had with his kindergarten teacher. Eventually, he will go to the team for special education testing, probably due to his behavior issues. This will inevitably classify him as an 'at-risk' Black student who will not measure up to school standards.

Jay moves up (barely) to first grade at Grayson and is placed in my class. He is always so cheerful and happy, even though he's at the bottom of the class academically. He enjoys reading and writing about severe weather conditions, especially hurricanes, tornadoes and earthquakes, and is passionate on all things weather related. He has three interventions in my classroom, all with the parents present or on the phone. We develop a plan for him to succeed in the classroom, and it's working to some degree. I set him up with a free community tutor, who comes to see him during the school day once a week, usually bringing some new book on extreme weather. He also participates in reading academic intervention, which helps with his decoding issues, and is a member of a boy's group (run through the school social worker). I also work with him a lot, before and after school and at lunch, and he participates in my after school chess club. As a mother of a child with a reading disability, I see the signs that this may be Jay's problem as well. I speak to the parents and push to have him evaluated for a reading disability. By the end of first grade nothing has occurred, but I am told he will be evaluated with the parent's permission in the beginning of second grade.

In second grade Jay moves upstairs to a multi-age inclusion classroom (1/2). Ms. Springstein, his kindergarten teacher, sends me regular picture updates on Jay, and the first thing I notice is his dramatic haircut. His long braids are gone. Now you can see his cute face with his deep dimples. According to the second grade teacher, Jay has caught up in his reading (decoding skills) and is now able to read on grade level. However, he still works very slowly, does not complete his work and has focus issues. The special education teacher in the room, as he is placed in an inclusion class, has unofficially diagnosed him with ADHD and says that his focus is getting worse. He has not been sent to the team and no parent interventions have occurred. At the parent teacher conferences, which the father has attended, the teachers have both relayed their concerns on his lack of focus. Now the teachers feel the ball is in the parent's court and he should be tested and medicated for this disorder.

Jay is moving up to third grade next year, the same inclusion classroom that Lina is presently in this year. He still smiles and hugs you when he sees you and he still loves to read and write about extreme weather. "He is going to be a meteorologist one day," says his second grade teacher. And he smiles. Later, outside in the hallway, the teacher makes it clear to me that Jay may not even make it to middle school, let alone be a meteorologist. I tell her to send me a picture of him in third, fourth and fifth grade, as I know I am invested in seeing that he makes it to middle school, so he can continue his weather studies.

Michael, who has an older sibling in the school as well, moves up to first grade without a problem. He's a very quiet student who does not get into trouble, so it's easy for him to fly under the radar for a while. He is placed in Ms. Franklin's multi-age, the same year she says she has multiple behavior problems and forgets about Lina entirely. She has no real recollection of Michael either; she just remembers he is quiet. After speaking to Ms. Watson, his kindergarten teacher, I realize that he is gone in the wind. She says the whole family moved out of the district and back to the nearby metropolitan area, where the schools are not as good. When I ask her why, she isn't sure, but it probably has to do with the rising cost of rent in the area.

Interestingly, in our conversation, Ms. Watson still focuses on the fact that he was absent too much in kindergarten and how that negatively affects a child's schooling process. She will forever remember him as lying to her about being sick and being behind in his work because of his absences. She blames the mother (see Chapter 5) and feels that he could have been more ready for school if he had been present in class more. The middle of the year slide to her relates to his mom's lack of effort. She judges her value system and sees very little future for Michael because of it. Valuing education, to her, is the key to the child's success, and Michael's mom just doesn't care.

I do not know exactly where Michael is right now at the end of second grade, but if he is in the nearby metropolitan district, he may not ever be heard, seen or noticed at all. Class sizes are large there and services are minimal. His talent for math could easily be overlooked, and he may never find his academic groove. His mom may continue to take him out of school, and as such he could have an attendance or lateness problem, which always negatively affects the teacher's perception of the child and their family.

The stigma of being identified as non-school ready has negatively affected all five children. It has followed them into their next class placement and it will stay with them even when they have caught up to their peers in reading (Lina and Jay). The deficit perception is teacher made and teacher perpetuated. An example of this is Jay, who although he is doing much better in reading, is still seen as non-school ready because he doesn't finish his work on time and has focus issues. Medication, diagnoses, testing, interventions and academic supports are all tools that are both helpful and harmful. Helpful, because some children need extra support and services, and harmful because they are just fulfilling their destinies of being non-school ready and therefore outside the normative structures of the school system.

A Call for Action

Now that I have critically examined the concept of *school readiness* and how it negatively impacts the daily lives of low-income Black children, it is time to propose a future action plan. It is not enough to deconstruct *school readiness* discourse and describe the hardships on low-income Black children. There needs to be a call to action, a way to empower these students and work with them within the system.

As described above, the issue of the macroeconomic local climate must be addressed first. Then the local school district must come to terms with their diverse populations and be more willing to attend to their needs. The following is a letter to a local school district (it could be Grayson's district or anywhere where there are high populations of young low-income Black children).

Dear local school district,

We need to stop utilizing the term/concept of *school readiness*. Research has shown (Booth & Crouter, 2008; Grau, 1993; Iorio & Parnell, 2015; Tager, 2015) that this term is detrimental to a child's learning trajectory. Most if not all children that are labeled with this deficit-based term are low-income non-White students. This just further segregates our school system and increases the numbers of suspensions, expulsions, drop-out rates, teen pregnancy and special education testing. Right now there are too many low-income Black children in special education programs or inclusion classrooms. They are also retained too much, which means they are behind their age appropriate peers. They are syphoned off at an early age, largely due to the perception of a teacher that believes they are non-school ready. And when they are outside the normative structures of the school, regular education, they are tracked into low-level positions. Even if they make it through all twelve grades, they may be at the bottom of the class. They are not tracked for college, but are instead bound for vocational training or the army. All of this tracking starts with the identification/classification of the non-school ready child in kindergarten and first grade.

What can we, as early childhood educators do about this? We must be critically aware of what we are doing in the classroom. We need to examine our expectations. Are they based on White middle class discourse? Are we even aware of other cultures in our classroom? Are we being culturally responsive? Do we utilize an authentic multicultural curriculum that includes anti-bias activities that challenge stereotypes?

This is an educational problem that will not go away unless we face it head on. We are contributing, unknowingly and knowingly, to the failure of the low-income Black child. We must take responsibility for our actions and change them.

What can you do, at the local district? You can ban this terminology. A good way to do this is to cut down on standardized testing. High stakes testing comes at a price, and low-income Black children are paying the most of this price. If you have to have tests, as they are mandated by the state and tied to funding, then view them differently. They do not need to be prepared for in kindergarten and first grade. Put the blocks, puppets and other play activities back into the curriculum. Do not expect or define a child's ability to learn by how long they can sit at a desk. This is not developmentally appropriate and should not be imposed on young children.

And why do children need to read in kindergarten? Back in my day (the 1970s), no one was expected to be reading in kindergarten. The pushing down of the curriculum, due to increased standards (Common Core) and high stakes testing, has changed this expectation, and it is not reasonable. The *Washington Post* published an article (Strauss 2015) entitled "Requiring kindergartners to read as Common Core does—May Harm Some." This article states that forcing young children to read can actually be harmful, as it is not necessarily developmentally appropriate at a kindergarten level. The author cites varies studies, including the report (put out by *The Alliance of Childhood) Reading ink: Little to Gain and Much to Lose* (2014), which posits that there is no evidence to support the belief that children who read earlier (in pre-k and kindergarten) achieve more academic success later on. Actually the report shows that there are greater gains related to children in play-based programs.

How can local school districts help to abolish this deficit-based term? First of all, schools need smaller class sizes. They need more teachers in the room (including aides, paraprofessionals and other support staff) so that there is a lower teacher-child ratio. A kindergarten class (like three in my study) with twenty-three children and one teacher in the room is an unacceptable practice. This practice directly affects how much time and attention teachers can give to their neediest students, and it gives them very little possibility of reaching all the students in the class. Developmentally appropriate practices for this age group call for two certified teachers for a class this size and a paraprofessional in the room. Early childhood classrooms (pre-k, kindergarten and first grade) should be capped at eighteen children or less.

Another problem that must be addressed is the local district adding to the curriculum. Let's be clear. There is no more instructional time in the day. Early childhood educators already have too much material to cover in a day. If you add something you must remove something. This is common sense. Utilizing three writing units is much more child friendly to a child that has issues with writing than seven writing units in a year. We cannot expect young children to produce more and more and more. Schools are not factories, and they need to be about the process of learning, not the product of learning. Teachers also need more flexibility in their schedule. They need time to put on a fairy puppet show, or produce a musical theater production. They need time for art, dance, sports, music and other activities outside the Common Core. Please note, that if you do not give them this flexibility, teachers will continue to have two different schedules, one fake one for the office and one real one for their classrooms.

You also need to address poverty issues in your school district. If there are Title One schools located in your district, you must constantly be thinking of ways to provide equitable resources to these schools. This means providing more district funds to these schools, with the realization that they can't fundraise like schools that have largely middle class families. It also means that the district must support the low-income families in their district by providing flexibility in times for parental involvement (and be aware of these parents' busy work schedules). This can mean that schools will hold their PTO meetings in the mornings before work or on the weekends. It is also imperative that the local school district provides food for the community. Schools in poor areas should provide dinners and brunches related to academic endeavors (i.e., family math night, etc.). Teachers in these schools need to go out into the local community and visit important facilities (community centers, senior centers, parks, libraries) and attend local community events. District personnel also need to be physically present in these local schools and attend all community functions, so that the families know that this particular school, even if it is not in a so-called good area of town, is an important learning environment.

It is also important to acknowledge that this continual practice of classifying non-school ready children and eventually syphoning out of the regular education classroom is racist and perpetuates racist behavior/practices in our society. In all of the classrooms where I did my study, there was only one White child labeled as non-school ready (out of 113 students in five classrooms). The rest are all self-identified as Black (including: Haitians, Africans, African Americans, West Indians and mixed race). This means that the district itself must be aware of this ongoing prejudicial practice. Teachers in this district and in all districts must be exposed to countless hours of professional development workshops relating to race and local culture. Perhaps with more self-awareness, half of these children would not be automatically labeled as deficient but instead would be recognized for their strengths and what they contribute positively to the classroom.

Please consider the above ideas and options when evaluating and reforming your school district policies and practices.

Thank you,
On behalf of all Early Childhood Educators past, present and future.

A call for action to reconceptualize how we think about early childhood education is critical at this point in history. It is time to rethink policies that are deficit-based and racist (NCLB, Race to the Top) and reimagine a more inclusive environment for all of our young children, especially low-income Black children, who have been excluded for so long.

It is important that future research critically challenge early childhood education deficit discourses. Such studies, like my own, need to be recognized by the larger early childhood community as one of many legitimate contributions to scholarly research. I am referring specifically to the international organization RECE (Reconceptualizing Early Childhood Education). Such research studies include: Bloch et al. (2014), Cannella (1997), Wright (2014) and more. In *Reconceptualizing Early Childhood Care and Education: A Reader*, Bloch addresses the important connection between critical research and political action. Reimagining early childhood education is in itself a political action. After twenty plus years of committing to the idea of reconceptualizing early childhood practices/pedagogy, these researchers (including myself) believe that this is an emancipatory process that challenges dominant discourses and provides alternative views of related power discourses. In this tradition I challenge the dominant discourse of *school readiness* and call for a reimagined view of this term, or the banning of this term, in order to fight against racism and deficit thinking surrounding low-income Black populations.

Educational Policy and Reform

It is important that the United States as a whole and the individual local school districts focus on the true purpose of early childhood education. Schools and programs need to focus on providing access to quality education for all of their young children.

In Finland, high stakes testing is no longer utilized on the national level (except for one test at the end of high school), and this country continues to be rated as one of the top educational systems in the world (Shaw, 2012). In her newspaper article, "Finland's educational success story: Less testing, more trusting," Shaw describes a nation, unlike the United States, where teaching is a top tiered respected profession and there is less homework and more outside time (Shaw, 2012). Clearly, more testing is not the answer. Instead, Finland does not require schooling until the age of seven, yet preschool is publically funded and available for all populations. The lack of testing and the universal option of preschool completely eradicates the need for school readiness identification.

Universal preschool is a viable option for the United States. All young children need the same access to quality preschool. This is not occurring, largely due to lack of funding. Nationally, bills that advocate for universal preschool have been discarded as not worthy.

In the 1970s, Senator Mondale sponsored the first ever comprehensive child development bill. It would have provided billions of dollars of federal funds to organize a universal preschool plan for the United States. The house and the senate both passed this bill, but President Nixon later vetoed it. He reasoned that:

> Good public policy requires that we enhance rather than diminish both parental authority and parental involvement with children . . . for the federal government to plunge head long financially into supporting child development would commit the vast moral authority of the natural government to the side of communal approaches to childrearing over and against the family-centered approach. This president is unwilling to take this step.
>
> (Joffe, 1977, p. xi)

This statement, made by a standing president of the United States, just reaffirms the heteronormative family discourse that imposes one cultural norm onto other populations. This has been the problem all along, as ideas of family and motherhood have been set up into binaries of good and bad. The good mother stays home and the bad mother leaves their child with strangers and goes to work. This normative discourse re-affirms the heterosexual nuclear family and the gender roles to be played out within this normative family structure.

There is an important issue that must be addressed that relates to setting up a universal preschool program. Unlike Finland, the United States is a nation full of diverse populations of preschoolers. Thus, the notion of universal must be challenged and critically analyzed. Universal as a term means that the same pedagogical practices/curriculum will be utilized in every preschool nationally. This is problematic, if applied, when the local cultural context of the preschool center/program is not considered. The local community needs to be a large part of the design of a preschool center. Otherwise, the dominant practices of schooling, based on White middle class values, will prevail in preschool. In order to do away with the *school readiness* agenda, early childhood educators must be attuned to the local culture of their preschool. Preschool is not just a place to learn the same school ready skills, it is a place of learning and co-construction and a place where children can explore and experience materials. Therefore, it must be noted that if the plan is to utilize universal preschool in order to make children more school ready, then I am opposed to this plan. If however, universal preschool is designed to meet the specific needs for local populations of preschoolers and is equally accessible to all populations, then it is a great method to combat deficit discourse related to the identification and classification of *school readiness*.

We also need a call for action to all professors of pre-service early childhood teachers. This needs to begin in the college classrooms. Teachers, who are at this time predominately White and female, have an obligation to learn about the deficit impact of labeling children as non-school ready. They need to be more aware of their own biases and ideas about different cultures.

This is not an easy task and will take a huge re-structuring of many early childhood programs. In order for this to truly work, there needs to be a concerted effort to hire more Black and Latina professors, so that these White educators are exposed to their own racism/biases. This, along with new and improved professional development workshops for White professors, will help to expose this undercurrent of prejudicial discourse.

As stated before, testing and higher demands on very young children are a considerable problem in the United States. I believe there isn't any need for testing/paper assessments in the early childhood classroom. Instead, we should practice holistic assessments based on performance and exploration through learning. For example, when a teacher observes a young child playing, they have a better understanding of how the child learns. They can see their strengths and their weaknesses in their play activities with others. This type of holistic assessment is much more appropriate for a young child. Paper and pencil assessments should be banned and no longer an everyday practice. As a long time early childhood educator, I remember in the 1990s when holistic/performance-based assessments and children's portfolios were the trend. I feel you learn a lot more from observation, reflection and from analyzing their finished work than you do from a paper assessment. New teachers will need training in this new and improved approach, but it's worthwhile in the end. Young children, such as Derek, Jay, Lina, Billy and Michael, will no longer feel the pressure of mandated tests in kindergarten and first grade. Overall, they and other children that are having trouble adapting to the school culture will have more space to grow and learn at their own pace.

Finally, it is important to note that new educational policy, both federally and locally funded, must be created and designed by the experts, early childhood educators that are presently in the field. Politicians and business CEOs have no place in the design of early childhood policy. Therefore, early childhood experts, as it stands now, must revamp the Common Core. Teachers in the field understand what is realistically appropriate to ask a young child to do. We need to utilize the experts, including early childhood doctoral students and professors in the field. I think we have lost sight of the importance of the early childhood educator. We can't just ask them to implement new policy after new policy that negatively affects their own pedagogical practices.

Future policy must be organized and created within a positive framework, one that is not deficit-based and racist in structure. Our policies reflect our great nation. They need to be democratic, inclusive and meet the needs of all of the populations presently living in the country.

Conclusion

School Readiness is currently utilized as a term that perpetuates a deficit racist ideology within early childhood programs. Discourses on the Common Core, standardized testing and the human capital of young children all filter this deficit at-risk concept and further segregate our low-income Black children. Unreal expectations, as defined by this agenda, further exacerbate this issue. *School readiness,* as a term, needs to be eradicated from the normative paradigm of early childhood education. It is tied directly to standardized testing practices/assessments that are not developmentally appropriate for five and six-year-olds. Therefore testing/assessments at this higher level should not be utilized in early childhood. The DRA testing is an example of this (refer to Table 4.1) and should not be utilized at all in kindergarten (except maybe as a baseline).

This call for action requires true educational reform, as noted in this chapter. This means that we need to reconceptualize early childhood pedagogical practices in general, but particularly in relation to deficit racist ideologies like *school readiness.* This is an ongoing journey and requires authentic reform both in and out of early childhood programs. The local community is also a key part of this action plan. School districts, such as the one in this study, must be aware and a part of their local school neighborhoods. Fostering Funds of Knowledge and mutual respect within the community will aid in getting rid of stigmas and deficit thinking.

Furthermore, local, state and federal policies must change. Policies, such as NCLB and Race to the Top, represent neoliberal ideologies and are ultimately detrimental to low-income Black children who are already outside the system. New educational policies that directly combat racism and deficit practices need to be created and put into place. Educator training in anti-bias curriculum, funds of knowledge and multicultural education should be a mandatory part of a nation-wide policy agenda.

Ultimately, the only recourse in challenging a deficit approach is to encourage and empower a child's own culture within the structure of the early childhood classroom. Lisa Delpit argues, "Go deny students their own expert knowledge is to disempower them" (Delpit, 2006, p. 33). This means that White teachers have to recognize and be aware of cultural differences within their Black populations and more importantly need to celebrate the different knowledges and cultural systems that are a fundamental part of these children's everyday lives. Empowerment is the key. However, it can't only be White people empowering low-income Black children. As I stated earlier, there must be a higher population of non-White early childhood educators within early childhood programs for this to fully work.

In order to do all of the above, in a call for action plan, we, as early childhood educators, need to be aware of what the identification/classification is actually doing to our non-White populations. And the first step in this is to ban *school readiness* as a term in early childhood practices. The next step is awareness/reflection on fundamentally racist structures that work within our classrooms, even without our knowledge. This is imperative for a workforce that is over 85% White and middle class. Reflection and challenging one's own biases creates a better teacher all around, but it also helps the child who is identified as non-school ready. Seeing other perspectives and thinking outside of our own dominant culture is paramount to a deeper understanding of the deficit nature of our identifications of *school readiness*.

Since this book begins with a narrative about Lina, I think it is only appropriate to end with another story of Lina and how this classification of being non-school ready follows her wherever she goes.

Lina walks into her classroom and goes right to the coat rack and bends down so no one can see her. What is she doing? After a while she emerges in all pink from her head to her toes. Her shirt says "smile" and even her sneakers are pink. Ms. Franklin walks over to her and places her hands with care on Lina's face.

"What I want you to do is go to your seat and finish illustrating," she is giving her private directions. When Lina moves too slowly toward her table Ms. Franklin says,

"You know what Lina . . . you need to finish," and she sits down in a chair next to Lina who is standing and coloring in her map.

"Let's help Lina get caught up," she says to a girl who cries a lot.

"You can just copy mine," says the crying girl. They are coloring in maps of the United States of America.

Lina presses very hard on the crayons as she colors. Her hair is neatly up in braids. She is very small next to the crier. Ms. Franklin leaves the area.

"It's 10:30 . . . two more minutes," she shouts to the class.

Lina has been in the room less than five minutes now.

"Come over to Writer's Workshop," Ms. Franklin instructs.

"I need more pink," Lina says to the crying girl and she digs around in the crayon bin in the middle of the table.

"You need purple," directs the crying girl.

"Uh-uh," and Lina shakes her head no firmly.

"I am helping you," says crying girl.

All the other children are now at the rug waiting.

"—and Lina . . . it's time," Ms. Franklin calls from the rug. Lina hurries to try and finish her map. She bends now and tries to work faster, her map is half finished. Finally she drops the pink crayon and rushes over to her rug spot. The work is unfinished on the table.

Lina, like Derek, Billy, Jay and Michael, will never catch up. They will remain outside the system and their work will be unfinished and their education undone. The above observation is a clear example of how children who are classified as non-school ready are isolated, stigmatized and are in a losing race in which they will never come out ahead. Leonard argues that "race is no longer only a variable to be plugged into a research study but rather a dynamic that saturates the entire schooling process" (Leonardo, 2013, p. 3). My hope is that this research contributes to this new view of race and education. Racism is reinforced and reproduced within early childhood institutions. It is implicated in every aspect of the pedagogical practices of early childhood educators, schools and districts at large. If we, as early childhood researchers/educators, do not make these taken for granted practices visible, we are in effect in collusion with the inherently racist structure of schooling.

Radical change and true awareness of this issue must occur in order to disrupt this deficit classification of young Black children. It is our turn now to hear the call for action and rise up, as early childhood educators, and demand a change. This change is personal and political and must be activated within all of us. Disruption of deficit practices comes from this activation and requires steadfast reflection and perseverance. Breaking the historical cycle related to this taken for granted practice takes hard work and conviction, but we are up for the challenge. No child (including Black children) should be identified as non-school ready anymore. Instead we must look to their strengths, incorporating local cultural contexts, and see the child for himself. Perhaps then we can see ourselves for who we really are too.

References

Adair, J. K. (2014). Agency and expanding capabilities in early grade classrooms: What it could mean for young children, in *Harvard Educational Review, 84 (2)*, pp. 217–241.

Allen, E. J. (2008). *Policy discourses, gender and education: Constructing women's status*. New York: Routledge.

Ames, L. & Ellsworth, J. (1997). *Women reformed, women empowered: Poor mothers and the endangered promise of Head Start*. Philadelphia, PA: Temple University Press.

Anyon, J. (2005). *Radical possibilities: Public policy, urban education and a new social movement*. New York: Routledge.

Apple, M. (1993). *Official knowledge: Democratic education in a conservative age*. New York: Routledge.

Apple, M. (2001). *Educating the 'right' way: Markets, standards, god and inequality*. New York: Routledge.

Bailey, E. (March, 2015). Postcolonial 'pre-conditioning': Understanding the academic achievement gap between White and minority students in the USA, in *Journal of Education and Social Policy, 2 (1)*, pp. 1–7.

Barnett, W. S. (1998). Long term effects on cognitive development and school success, In S. Barnett & S. S. Boocock (Eds.) *Early care and education for children in poverty: Promises, programs and long term results*, pp. 11–44. Albany, NY: SUNY Press.

Barnett, W. S. & Boocock, S. S. (Eds.) (1998). *Early care and education for children in poverty: Promises, programs and long term results*. Albany, NY: State University of New York Press.

Beatty, B. (1995). *Preschool education in America: The culture of young children from the colonial era to the present*. New Haven: Yale University Press.

Becker, G. (1994). *Human capital: A theoretical and empirical analysis, with special reference to education* (3rd edition). Chicago: University of Chicago Press.

Bloch, M. N., et al. (2014). *Reconceptualizing early childhood care and education: A reader*. New York: Peter Lang.

Bloom, B. (1964). *Stability and change in human characteristics*. New York: Wiley Publishing.

Bloom, B., et al. (1965). *Compensatory education for cultural deprivation*. New York: Holt, Rinehart & Winston.

Bonilla-Silva, E. (2006). *Racism without racists: Color-blind racism and the persistence of racial inequality in the U.S.* (2nd edition). Rowman & Littlefield Publishing.

Booth, A. & Crouter, A. (Eds.) (2008). *Disparities in school readiness: How families contribute to transitions into school*. New York: Lawrence Erlbaum Associates.

Bredekamp, S. & Copple, C. (1997). *Developmentally appropriate practice in early childhood programs.* Washington, DC: NAEYC.

Burman, E. (2007). *Deconstructing developmental psychology* (2nd edition). New York: Routledge.

Cannella, G. (1997). *Deconstructing early childhood education: Social justice and revolution.* New York: Peter Lang.

Chappell, D. (Ed.) (2010). *Children under construction: Critical essays on play as curriculum.* New York: Peter Lang.

Charmez, K. (2014). *Constructing grounded theory.* New York: Sage Publications. www.CNN.com (front page) June 17th, 2015, retrieved July 2016.

Cowie, B. & Carr, M. (2004). The consequences of socio-cultural assessment, In A. Anning et al. (Eds.) *Early childhood education: Society and culture.* London: Sage Publishing.

Danielson, C. (2007). *Enhancing professional practice: A framework for teaching.* Virginia: Association for Supervision and Curriculum Development.

Davis, M. (1933). Business meetings—Proceedings of the 6th conference of the National Association for Nursery Education.

Delpit, L. (2006). *Other people's children: Cultural conflict in the classroom.* New York: New Press.

Devault, M. (2008). *People at work: Life, power and social inclusion in the new economy.* New York: New York University Press.

Diangelo, R. (2012). *What does it mean to White? Developing White racial literacy.* New York: Peter Lang.

Dodson, L. (2009). *The moral underground: How ordinary Americans subvert an unfair economy.* New York: New Press.

Edwards, D. (1999). Public factors that contribute to school readiness, in *Early Childhood Research and Practice, 1 (2),* pp. 1–5.

Ehrenreich, B. (2011). *Nickel and dimed: On (not) getting by in America* (10th Anniversary edition). New York: Picador.

Ehrenreich, B. & Hochschild, A.R. (Eds.) (2004). *Global women: Nannies, maids and sex workers in the new economy.* New York: Henry Holt.

Emerson, R.M., et al. (2011). *Writing ethnographic field notes* (2nd edition). Chicago: University of Chicago Press.

Epstein, J., et al. (ed). (2009). *School, family and community partnerships: Your handbook for action.* London: Sage Publishing.

Erikson, E.H. (1950). *Childhood and society.* New York: W.W. Norton.

Fantuzzo, J., et al. (Fall, 2004). Multiple dimensions of family involvement and their relations to behavioral and learning competencies for urban, low-income children, in *School Psychology Review, 33 (4).*

Ferguson, A. (2001). *Bad boys: Public schools and the making of Black masculinity.* Michigan: University of Michigan Press.

Frankenberg, R. (1993). *White women, race matters: The social construction of whiteness.* Minneapolis, MN: University of Minnesota Press.

Gillborn, D. (2008). *Racism and education: Coincidence or conspiracy?* New York: Taylor and Francis.

Grau, E. (1993). *Ready for what? Constructing meanings of readiness for kindergarten.* Albany: SUNY Press.

Gupta, A. (2006). Early experiences and personal funds of knowledge and beliefs of immigrant and minority teacher candidates dialog with theories of child development in a teacher education classroom, in *Journal of Early Childhood Teacher Education, 27,* pp. 3–18.

Hale, J. (2001). *Learning while Black: Creating educational excellence for African American children.* Baltimore, MD: John Hopkins University Press.

Hale-Benson, J. & Hilliard, A. (1986). *Black children: Their roots, culture and learning styles*. Baltimore, MD: John Hopkins University Press.

Harry, B. & Klingner, J. (2006). *Why are so many minority students in special education? Understanding race and disability in schools*. New York: Teachers College Press.

Harvey, D. (1989). *The condition of postmodernity*. Boston, MA: Blackwell Publishing.

Harvey, D. (2005). *A brief history of neoliberalism*. New York: Oxford University Press.

hooks, b. (1994). *Teaching to transgress: Education as the practice of freedom*. New York: Routledge.

Hunt, J. M. (1961). *Intelligence and experience*. New York: Ronald Press.

Iorio, J. M. & Parnell, W. (2015). *Rethinking readiness in early childhood education: Implications for policy and practice*. New York: Palgrave Macmillan.

Joffe, C. (1977). *Friendly intruders: Childcare professionals and family life*. Berkeley, CA: University of California Press.

Jordan, B. (2009). Scaffolding learning and co-constructing understandings, In A. Anning et al. (Eds.) *Early childhood education: Society and culture*. London: Routledge.

Keddie, N. (Ed.) (1973). *The myth of cultural deprivation*. New York: Penguin Education.

Keeley, B. (2007). *Human capital: The power of knowledge*. New York: OCED.

Konald, T. & Pianta, R. (2005). Empirically derived person oriented patterns of school readiness in typically developing children: Description and prediction to first grade achievement, in *Applied Developmental Science*, 9, pp. 174–187.

Labov, W. (1973). The logic of nonstandard English, In N. Keddie (Ed.) *The myth of cultural deprivation* (pp. 21–67). New York: Penguin Education.

Lara-Cinisomo, S., et al. (2004). *Are L.A.'s children ready for school?* Santa Monica, CA: Rand Corporation.

Lareau, A. (2003). *Unequal childhoods: Class, race and family life*. Berkeley, CA: University of California Press.

Lareau, A. & Weininger, E. B. (2008). The context of school readiness: Social class differences in time use in family life, In A. Booth & A. C. Crouter (Eds.) *Disparities in school readiness: How families contribute to transitions into school* (pp. 155–189). New York: Lawrence Erlbaum Associates.

Lee, W., et al. (2013). *Understanding the Te Wharki approach: Early years education in practice*. London: Routledge.

Leonardo, Z. (2009). *Race, whiteness and education*. New York: Routledge.

Leonardo, Z. (2013). *Race frameworks: A multidemensional theory of racism and education*. New York: Teachers College Press.

Linder, S., Ramey, M. and Zambak, S. (2013). Predictors for school readiness in literacy and mathematics: A selective review of the literature, in *Early Childhood Research & Practice, 15 (1)*, pp. 1–9.

Lubeck, S. (2001). The role of culture in program improvement, in *Early Childhood Research Quarterly, 16*, pp. 499–523.

Luttrell, W. & Dodson, L. (Winter, 2011). Families faring untenable choices, in *Contexts, 10 (1)*, pp. 38–52.

Macintyre, C. (2016). *Enhancing learning through play: A developmental perspective* (3rd edition). New York: Routledge.

MacNaughton, G. (2005). *Doing Foucault in early childhood studies: Applying poststructural ideas*. London: Routledge.

Martusewicz, R., et al. (2011). *Eco justice education: Toward diverse, democratic and sustainable communities*. New York: Routledge.

Massey, D. & Denton, N. (1993). *American apartheid: Segregation and the making of the underclass*. Cambridge, MA: Harvard University Press.

Meier, D., et al. (Eds.) (2004). *Many children left behind*. Boston: Beacon Press.

Mercado, C. (2005). Seeing what's there: Language and literacy funds of knowledge in New York Puerto Rican homes, In A. Zentella (Ed.) *Building on strength: Languages and literacy in Latino families and communities*. New York: Teachers College Press.

Moses, R. & Cobb, C.E. (2002). *Radical equations: Civil rights from Mississippi to the Algebra Project*. Boston: Beacon Press.

Moynihan, D.P. (1964). The negro family: A case for national action, In L. Rainwater & W. Yancy (Eds.) *The Moynihan report and the politics of controversy* (pp. 39–125). Cambridge, MA: MIT Press.

NAEYC (2009). Mission statement of developmentally appropriate practices. www.naeyc.com

OCED (2007). *Human capital: How what you know shapes your life*. Danvers, MA: OCED Publications.

Parks, N. (2014). *Exploring mathematics through play in the early Childhood class*. New York: Teacher's College Press.

Pearl, A. (1997). Cultural and accumulated environmental deficit models, In R.R. Valencia (Ed.) *The evolution of deficit thinking: Educational thought and practice* (pp. 132–160). New York: Routledge.

Penn, H. (2008). *Unequal childhoods: Young children's lives in poor countries*. London: Routledge.

Polakow, V. (2007). *Who cares for our children? The childcare crisis in the other America*. New York: Teachers College Press.

Postman, N. (1973). The politics of reading, In N. Keddie (Ed.) *The myth of cultural deprivation* (pp. 86–96). New York: Penguin Education.

Rainwater, L. & Yancy, W. (1967). *The Moynihan report and the politics of controversy*. Cambridge, MA: MIT Press.

Ramey, C. & Ramey, S. (2004). Early learning and school readiness: Can early intervention make a difference? in *Merrill-Palmer Quarterly, 50*, pp. 471–491.

Randolph, A. (2013). *The wrong kind of different: Challenging the meaning of diversity in American classrooms*. New York: Teachers College Press.

Ravitch, D. (2010). *The death and life of the great American school system: How testing and choice are undermining education*. New York: Basic Bks.

Riessman, F. (1962). *The culturally deprived child*. New York: Harper & Row.

Robinson, K. & Harris, A. (2014). *The broken compass: Parental involvement with children's education*. Cambridge, MA: Harvard University Press.

Rock, D.A. & Stenner, A.J. (Spring, 2006). Assessment issues in the testing of children at school entry, in *The Future of Children—School Readiness: Closing Racial and Ethnic Gaps, 15 (1)*, pp. 15–35.

Roediger, D. (2005). *Working toward whiteness: How America's immigrants became White*. New York: Basic Books.

Rogers, S. (Ed.) (2010). *Rethinking play and pedagogy in early childhood education: Concepts, contexts and cultures*. London: Routledge.

Roosevelt, F. Address to the Nation (1930s) over the radio.

Ryan, W. (1976). *Blaming the victim* (2nd edition). New York: Vintage Press.

Shaw (November, 2012). Finland's educational success story: Less testing, more trusting. www.seattletimes.com. Retrieved July, 2016.

Stack, C. (1975). *All our kin: Strategies for survival in a Black community*. New York: Harper and Row Publishers.

Steinfels, M. (1973). *Who's minding the children? The history and politics of day care in America*. New York: Simon & Schuster.

Strauss, A. & Corbin, J. (Eds.) (1997). *Grounded theory in practice*. London: Sage.

Strauss, V. (2015). Requiring kindergartners to read as Common Core does may harm some. www.washingtonpost.com.

Tager, M. (2015). Dissertation "The ecology of school readiness" CUNY Graduate Center.

U.S. Department of Education (2013–14 report). Office of Civil Rights. www2. ed.gov.

Valencia, R. (1997). *The evolution of deficit thinking: Educational thought and practice*. New York: Routledge.

Valencia, R. (2010). *Dismantling contemporary deficit thinking: Educational thought and practice*. New York: Routledge.

Valencia, R. & Solarzano, D. G. (1997). Contemporary deficit thinking, In R. Valencia (Ed.) *The evolution of deficit thinking: Educational thought and practice*. New York: Routledge.

Waugh, J. (1997). *Unsentimental reformer: The life of Josephine Shaw Lowell*. Cambridge, MA: Harvard University Press.

Wolfmeyer, M. (forthcoming 2017). *Mathematics education: A critical introduction*. New York: Routledge.

Wood, C. (2007). *Yardsticks: Children in the classroom, ages 4–14* (3rd edition). New York: Center for Responsive Schools.

World Bank (2003). *Lifelong learning in the global knowledge economy: Challenges for developing countries*. Washington, DC: World Bank.

Wright, J., et al. (2001). The relations of early television viewing to school readiness and vocabulary of children from low-income families: The early window project, in *Child Development, 72*, pp. 1347–1366.

Wright, T. (2014). Revisiting risk/re-thinking resilience: Fighting to live versus failing to thrive, In M. Bloch et al. (Eds.) *Reconceptualizing early childhood care and education: A reader* (pp. 183–193). New York: Peter Lang.

Wu, F. & Qi, S. (2006). Longitudinal effects of parenting on children's academic achievement in African American families, in *Journal of Negro Education, 75*, pp. 415–429.

www.ACLU.org (ACLU complaint against————). Retrieved October, 2014.

www.BostonGlobe.com (School PTO's play key role in technology funding). Retrieved January, 2014.

Zigler, E. (2006). *Vision for a universal preschool education*. New York: Cambridge University Press.

Zigler, E. & Styfco, S. (2010). *The hidden history of Head Start*. New York: Oxford University Press.

Index

Made in the USA
Monee, IL
19 March 2021

63305506R00077